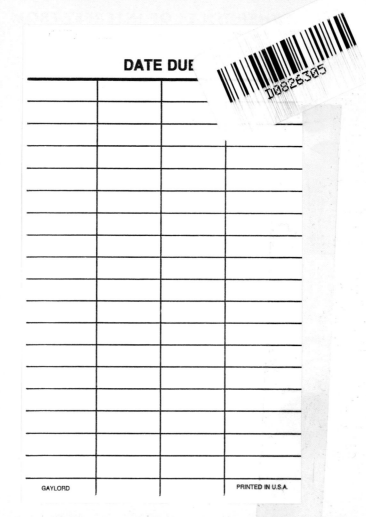

WRITE YOUR WAY INTO COLLEGE

COLLEGE ADMISSIONS ESSAY

OTHER TITLES OF INTEREST FROM LEARNINGEXPRESS

411 SAT Essay Prompts and Writing Questions
Grammar Success in 20 Minutes a Day
Write Better Essays in 20 Minutes a Day
Writing Skills Success in 20 Minutes a Day

WRITE YOUR WAY INTO COLLEGE

COLLEGE ADMISSIONS ESSAY

LEARNINGEXPRESS®

NEW YORK

Published in the United States by LearningExpress, LLC, New York.

Library of Congress Cataloging-in-Publication Data

Write your way into college : college admissions essay / Learning Express, LLC.
    p. cm.
  Includes bibliographical references.
  ISBN 978-1-57685-727-4
  1. College applications—United States. 2. Universities and colleges—United States—Admission. 3. Exposition (Rhetoric) 4. Essay—Authorship. I. LearningExpress (Organization)
  LB2351.52.U6W75 2010
808'.066378—dc22   2010004076

Printed in the United States of America

9 8 7 6 5 4 3 2 1

First Edition

ISBN 13: 978-1-57685-727-4

For information or to place an order, contact LearningExpress at:
  2 Rector Street
  26th Floor
  New York, NY 10006

Or visit us at:
  www.learnatest.com

Contents

CONTENTS

CONTENTS

Contributors

Lauren Starkey is an author, editor, and educator. She has written 20 books, including *How to Write Great Essays*, *SAT Writing Essentials*, *Goof Proof College Admissions Essays*, and test prep titles for the SAT, GRE, LSAT, and MCAT. Lauren created SAT Bootcamp—4 Hours to a Higher Score (www.satboot camp.us), a New England-based test strategy workshop that's now in its fourth year. She also writes a column on college admissions for www.examiner.com, and provides customized test prep and college essay counseling for individual students. Lauren lives in Vermont with her husband and three children.

Introduction ▶

This book is designed to guide students through the part of the college application that produces the most anxiety: the personal essay. The rest of the application, with the exception of teacher recommendations, is straightforward and objective—it asks for things like lists of activities, achievements, future plans, and background information. But the essay is different.

Hundreds of schools use the Common Application (www.commonapp.org), which offers a choice of six prompts, or essay topics. Even schools that don't accept the common application usually offer very similar prompts (see Appendix B for a list of colleges that accept the common application). However, even with essay topics to guide you, the response field is wide open. You can write about *anything* you want (although you'll learn in the chapters ahead why some subjects should be avoided). It's often this lack of restrictions that makes the personal essay so difficult to approach—many students believe that there is, among all the possibilities, "One Perfect Story," and if they fail to uncover it, the entire application will suffer.

But "One Perfect Story" isn't the only essay myth that often holds students back. Another is the myth of the "Well-Rounded Student." If you believe that the schools you're applying to are looking for do-it-all Renaissance students, you'll be tempted to cram everything you've done since your first day of freshman year into your essay. That can be a big mistake for two reasons.

First, it's not true that schools are only looking for athletic, musical, intellectual, do-gooders with perfect leadership skills who also manage to save puppies and write about it for the school newspaper. Second, if you try to cover too much ground your essay opportunity will be wasted. Instead of a personal piece that connects with the reader, you'll end up with a laundry list of accomplishments that have already been detailed elsewhere on your application.

This book will guide you along the path to writing an effective essay that *will* get you noticed. Once you understand what schools are looking for, you'll be able to mine your life for key experiences that reveal important things about you, and that will get a positive reaction from an admissions reader. You'll also learn what to avoid, and how to organize your writing for maximum impact. There will also be opportunities to practice making any prompt personal, which will help you avoid the number one admissions essay blunder—writing about anything and everything *instead* of yourself. Along the way, you'll get expert advice from admissions officers, college counselors, and students who have successfully made it through the admissions process. You'll also find answers to some of the most commonly asked questions about the admissions essay.

In the final chapters, you'll learn how to correct the most common errors in word choice, grammar, and mechanics. Since these errors are the ones often tested by the College Board on multiple-choice SAT writing questions, you'll not only learn how to improve your essay, but you'll be able to better answer questions on other sections of the SAT. Finally, you'll get to put what you've learned in this book to the test. Eight complete essays are included in chapter 8; it will be your job to decide what works, and what doesn't. Compare your notes to the professional feedback offered after each essay.

Don't forget, your personal essay is what makes your application come alive. As schools do away with interviews, and more and more students submit greater numbers of applications, it's one of the best ways to stand out and make a positive connection with admissions officers. Remember this as you write—they are looking to find intelligent and articulate students to accept. Appeal to them, and your essay can help you move one step closer to attending your first choice school!

1

WHAT IS A GREAT ESSAY, AND WHY IS IT SO IMPORTANT?

For the most part, filling out college applications isn't really difficult, although it does take time. Most of the information you are asked to provide is straightforward (address, birth date, Social Security number, siblings, etc.), and what you don't know you can easily look up. Then there's the essay. It's the piece that often turns the application from an hour of fill-in-the-blanks to weeks of nail-biting stress. But it doesn't have to be so stressful. When you understand the purpose of the essay, how to find a unique story worth telling, and what school admissions departments are looking for, you can write a great essay in just a few hours.

The personal essay has been a part of college applications since the 1920s. Designed to help admissions officers get a broader view of applicants, the essay, for most of its history, played a minor role in the decision-making process. However, in the last few decades, that role has changed significantly.

A number of things have made the essay a much more important factor in the admissions equation. There is increased competition as more students apply to a greater number of colleges. As a result, admissions officers must rely on factors such as the essay to differentiate among groups of students whose grades and test scores are very similar.

In addition, research studies are calling into question the validity of standardized tests like the SAT and ACT as predictors of success in college. Hundreds of schools have adopted test optional admissions policies, which means that students can opt to apply without having their SAT or ACT scores evaluated. The value of class rank has also been examined, resulting in thousands of high schools that no longer rank their students. Taken together, these trends have resulted in some of the less numbers-driven factors, such as teacher recommendations and the essay, to gain in importance.

You should view these developments as a positive development—who you are is just as important as your statistics. And there are a couple of other great reasons why the growing importance of the essay is something to get excited about. You're writing about the one subject you know better than anyone else—yourself. Also, you're in control. The truth is, by the time you write your essay you can't do much to improve your grades, test scores, extracurricular involvement, or relationships with your teachers. But with the essay, you're starting from scratch. With the help of this book, you can write an essay that makes a positive connection with your reader, and prompts him or her to place your application in the accepted pile!

Greater Admissions Competition

Across the country, record numbers of high school seniors are applying for a predetermined number of slots in the freshman classes of colleges and universities. By the end of the 20th century, 78 percent of colleges reported an increase in the number of applicants. According to the National Association of College Admissions Counselors, total college enrollment will continue to increase through 2016.

The actual number of applications that students are submitting is also rising, due to three significant factors. First, most schools now prefer (and some demand) the online submission of applications, which is often easier for students to complete. Second, the number of schools accepting the Common Application continues to rise. These factors make it much easier for students to apply to multiple schools. Instead of painstakingly filling out separate paper applications for each school, computer generated and submitted forms need only be completed once and tweaked slightly for each additional college.

Another factor is often referred to as the *snowball effect*. Because there are more students applying to more colleges, anxiety about getting accepted increases. This anxiety results in students applying to even more colleges in an effort to increase their chances of acceptance. The magic number of applications, according to conventional wisdom, used to be six. In the past, students were advised to apply to schools as follows: two *reach schools*—ones they wanted to attend but whose usual admissions standards were set above their grades and test scores; two *safety schools*—which were considered easy to be accepted by; and two other schools at which the probability of acceptance fell somewhere in the middle of those extremes.

However, as the number of students applying to schools increased, the rule of six became obsolete. According to UCLA's Higher Education Research Institute, the number of students applying to seven or more schools is currently around 20 percent, double what it was in 1990. Of course, all those applications have made it easier for schools to become more selective, rejecting many more students than they used to. So students respond by submitting even more applications, and the cycle continues.

Increasing Importance of the Essay

The National Association of College Admissions Counselors reports that the essay continues to gain in importance as a key admissions decision factor. Almost 25.8 percent of admissions counselors surveyed report the essay to be a considerable decision factor, a 100 percent increase since 1993. Over 64 percent report that the essay was a considerable or moderate factor, *exceeding* teacher recommendations, extracurricular activities, class rank, and the interview.

Because of increased competition and the likelihood that many of a school's applicants have very similar grades and test scores, it's important to have a part of your application that really stands out. What makes you stand out in high school—being the captain of the soccer team, student government president, or editor of your school newspaper perhaps—probably won't give you much of a true distinction in college admissions. Remember, there are over 40,000 public and private secondary schools in the country, which means that there are thousands of team captains, class presidents, and newspaper editors. Therefore, your essay is the perfect vehicle to express your unique personality and take on life—something that is uniquely yours!

Even schools that say grades and test scores are the most important admissions criteria can end up making key application decisions based on the essay. Consider that hundreds, if not thousands, of applicants to the same schools that you are applying to will have near identical grades and test scores. How do admissions committees make their decisions then? They use the essay as a *tip factor*: all other things being equal, they consider whose essay is better than the rest. In this scenario, it can easily become the reason for accepting or rejecting your application.

You're in the Driver's Seat

Here's something to consider: at this point in your academic career, your essay is the only piece of the admissions puzzle left which you've got complete control over. You can't go back and change your grades or recalculate your class rank. You've probably already taken the SAT or ACT. Your recommendations are likely completed. However, your essay has yet to be written. Use this opportunity to highlight something on your application that only got a brief mention, show admissions officers how much you want to attend their school(s), and explain what you'll bring to the school community that very few other students will.

Your essay can also balance your grades and test scores, especially if they fall below the median reported by the school(s) you're applying to. If this is the case, you'll need something on your application that makes you stand out from the crowd and helps to make up for any shortcomings. A great essay can do just that, within reason.

Many admissions departments use a rating system that separates academic achievement from personal, and the two scores are both considered. Boosting your personal rating will obviously improve your overall chances—but it won't produce a miracle. As college counselor Susan Goodkin explains:

> *"The students who will be helped most by a strong essay are the ones in the middle. If you're applying to a school that admits mostly students with 4.0s and near perfect test scores, and your numbers are much lower, an essay won't do much for you. The numbers will be the deciding factor. But if you're in the middle range, a great essay can really help."*

What is a Great Essay?

Now that we've established why you need one, what exactly makes an essay great? While there are variations in taste between admissions counselors, there are many points on which most agree.

It's All About You

A great essay should be personal. Many of the Common Application topics prompt you to explore something external, whether it's a work of art, a heroic figure, or an era in history. But your goal shouldn't be to write a term paper—it's to reveal something important about you. You don't need to sound like Hemingway, provide unique insight into the Obama administration, or explain why your high school's debate team should have won the National Championship.

The bottom line is that the essay is meant to give admissions officers an idea of who you are. Period. Do anything else with your essay, such as explain why Michael Jackson was the greatest entertainer of all time or why the life of Mother Teresa was inspiring, and you've blown your chance. Remember, schools are cutting back on interviews and record numbers of students are applying to college, so writing an essay that provides a glimpse of who you are is more important than ever.

ADVICE FROM A PRO

"I worked with one student who wrote an amazing essay about her father. It made me feel like I knew this man, who was a really incredible person. In fact, I'm sure the school she was applying to would have accepted him on the basis of that essay. But he wasn't the one applying. I suggested she start over, and keep the essay about herself."

—CHRIS AJEMIAN, CEO of CATES Tutoring, New York

Of course you will be judged on the quality of your writing. You'll need to show that you have a good grasp of language and essay development. But just as important is your message. Your essay must not only make you come alive, but also help your reader(s) to connect with you. Therefore, choosing your message—the story you tell about yourself—is as important as good grammar and vocabulary.

Focus

A strong essay also has a clear focus. It doesn't try to showcase everything you've achieved since your first day of freshman year. Most of that has been listed elsewhere on your application. With only about 500 words to tell your story, a lack of essay focus means that you'll end up with a laundry list rather than a personal, in-depth look at who you are. Here are some examples of essay topics and how they can be focused:

- **A volunteer position at a hospital.** Instead of a wide-ranging description of all the good you do (and to avoid sounding conceited), zero in on a positive interaction with one person, or one memorable aspect of your position.
- **A love of long distance running.** Ditch the cross-country team victories and defeats—they're not as personal as a description of what you see on your favorite route, what you listen to, or how running helps you stay centered.

- **An award-winning photography series.** Awards are already mentioned elsewhere on your application (as is the volunteer position and the cross-country team). Take this opportunity to discuss what you've learned by looking through the lens of your camera. Get specific—clichés not only bore readers but also ruins your chance to make a positive connection.

The Myth of the Well-Rounded Student

Many students fall into the laundry list trap because they mistakenly believe admissions committees are only looking for students who are extraordinarily well rounded. The myth of the well-rounded student may have started because of the large number of categories on most applications. There are places to list your academic, sports, music, leadership, work, and volunteer achievements. But the reality is that most students don't have things to brag about in every category. Instead, they focus on excelling in a few key interests.

What college admissions officers are really seeking is a well-rounded freshman class, not just a group of renaissance students who can do it all. In fact, long lists of varied activities can backfire and be interpreted as a warning sign: is the list of activities just a stab at impressing them, with busyness masking the fact that the student has no idea what he or she is really interested in?

Ron Moss (http://www.mycollegeguide.org/read/real.html), director of enrollment management at Southern Methodist University, speaks for hundreds of schools when he notes the variety of students he and his admissions committee are seeking:

> *"We need geniuses in our class to ensure academic pace. We need an occasional eccentric to balance our cynicism and remind us of our individuality. We need artists and musicians to represent the richness of our pilgrimage. We need leaders who can provide vision and inspiration. We need active members and doers who can make the vision come true. We need athletes and 4-Hers and math whizzes and ultimate frisbee and quiz bowl champs, and travelers of foreign lands, and givers of themselves."*

When you lose the urge to cover it all, you can use your essay to focus on something that's important to you and isn't already mentioned on your application, or something that's mentioned very briefly but is worth examining in

> ### HERE'S WHAT WORKED
>
> *"My daughter was accepted to a highly selective liberal arts school because of her unique resume, not in spite of it. In the admissions process she was able to sell herself based on the depth rather than the breadth of her passions."*
>
> —Mother of a sophomore at Vassar College

depth. Explaining what being on the tennis team means to you can be a waste of an opportunity. A great essay goes beyond this, and offers a glimpse of who you are—a person with passions, emotions, and a life beyond grades, test scores, and games.

Who is Your Audience?

No matter what you're writing, it's important to keep your audience in mind. The term paper you craft for your English class doesn't sound like a text message to a friend because you know the expectations of your audience. Writing an effective application essay is no different—you need to understand something about the people who evaluate them in an admissions department.

It's not easy to describe a typical admissions officer because most schools hire a diverse group of individuals: young and old, male and female, scholar and jock, conservative and liberal. However, some things they do have in common are an ability to spot good writing and a willingness to make a connection with their applicants. Your job is to try to appeal to one or more of them.

Average college admissions offices are staffed by between 10 and 20 people. However, some large universities, such as the University of Texas at Austin, can have up to 40 employees or more. There is usually a Dean, or Director of Admissions, who leads a team of Assistant or Associate Directors. Some schools even hire senior interns, who are still working toward their degrees, to evaluate applications.

Each admissions officer is typically in charge of a specific geographical area of the country, or even of the world if the school attracts, or wants to attract, a large number of international students. They travel to these target areas to attend college fairs, conduct interviews, and speak at secondary schools. They are available to applicants to answer questions and give a better idea of what the school they represent is like (especially if they are alumni).

When admissions applications are submitted, the work of the committee goes into high gear. Some schools receive hundreds or even thousands of applications for each spot in the freshman class.

INSIDER INFORMATION

Think admissions officers view essay reading as a dreaded chore? That's simply not the case. Augustine Garza, an admissions officer at the University of Texas–Austin, is representative of many professionals when he notes:

"At the end of the day, I find it refreshing to read that students still love their families, and that some of the major issues of our day matter to them. It gives me a clearer picture of what's going on in the minds of young people. And that I enjoy."

Others are less selective, but still must evaluate each application they receive. Everyone on the committee gets many essays to read, which often means they can spend an average of just a few minutes evaluating each one.

Admissions directors do not simply read essays with a highly judgmental eye, ready to circle every dangling participle or toss your essay if they find an unclear pronoun reference (but that doesn't mean you can skip the editing process). Instead, they look to find essays that they connect with. It can be that they sense, through your writing skills, that you are capable of handling a college workload, or that you'd be a great asset to their school's community.

What Not to Write

Because you're writing a personal essay, it's important to differentiate between what's appropriate and what you need to avoid. College counselor Chris Ajemian makes it simple:

> *"I tell my students to avoid the 4 D's: death, drugs, diseases, and disorders. To admissions officers, you're a potential investment in their school's future; you are more than your disorder or your disease. Allowing those things to define you can be limiting. Let them get to know you as a person in a broader sense."*

GREAT QUESTION!

"Everyone tells me I'm pretty funny. Should I use humor in my essay to connect with my readers?"

This is a tough question, and the simple answer is probably not. A light-hearted, witty tone is fine—if it fits with your subject. But resist the urge to tell a wild and crazy story, or to tell a straight story with jokes and puns thrown in. Remember, you don't know your reader's sense of humor. If he or she doesn't find it funny, you run the risk of looking foolish or being offensive. Susan Wertheimer, Senior Associate Director of Admissions at the University of Vermont, counsels:

"Funny is hard, and very few students can carry it off."

Even if you're known for your great sense of humor, keep your tone upbeat but leave out the jokes.

Admissions officers note that the worst essays usually fall into one or more of three categories:

- overly depressing or negative
- painting an unflattering picture of the applicant
- completely impersonal or unoriginal

They also report an increase in the number of these types of essays submitted. While there are a number of reasons why students are so revealing about negative aspects of themselves (i.e. discussing the influence of reality television, Facebook, and other outlets, where telling it all is encouraged, etc.), it's important to understand that the personal level that you use to communicate with friends is not appropriate for your essay. College counselor Susan Goodkin explains:

"Schools are really interested in students who are going to have a positive impact in their community. They don't want to be in the headlines because of something negative a student did. So think carefully about your essay. Your sense of privacy, probably because of Facebook, is different from an adult's. What's amusing or clever to your friends, like posting the lyrics to a dark song, can make an admissions officer cringe. Don't offer a reason to reject you by writing something dark. Keep your audience in mind at all times."

WHAT MAKES A GREAT APPLICATION ESSAY? A GREAT APPLICATION ESSAY:

- is personal.
- reveals something unique about you that readers can connect with.
- doesn't just repeat things already covered somewhere else on your application.
- is focused and doesn't try to cover too much ground.
- zeros in on key points.
- is well written and reflects your own voice.
- is free from spelling and grammar mistakes.
- isn't overly depressing, unflattering, or inappropriately revealing.

CHOOSING YOUR STORY— THE REVERSE APPROACH

Here's where many students get stuck: now that you know how important the essay is, and why you need it to be as good as it can be, what should you write about? The real roadblock lies in the misconception that there is one *perfect* story, and that if you don't determine what it is your essay won't be great. For every idea you come up with, a nagging doubt rises: "Is this *the* story, or is there a better one that I just haven't thought of yet?" That's the kind of thinking that can stop even professional writers in their tracks.

The reality is that there are likely dozens of worthy stories, and you can write a powerful personal essay on any one of them. In this chapter, we'll explore four effective brainstorming methods to help you uncover them. Using one or more of the following techniques can help you get over the feeling of being overwhelmed by the importance of this writing task, and move you closer toward crafting an effective admissions essay.

Why You Need to Brainstorm

You've been told about the importance of brainstorming in your English and Composition classes: jumping into an essay with no idea of where you're headed is almost always a waste of time and a bad idea (and this is especially true for

> ## GREAT QUESTION!
>
> *"What about the essay topics on my application? Don't I need to choose one first and then figure out what to write about?"*
>
> In a word—no. For many students, the best approach, and the one that guarantees that the story you want to tell gets told, is the reverse. First, determine what you want to say about yourself, and then choose a topic that works with your story. Remember that the Common Application offers a "Topic of Your Choice." Even schools that don't use the Common Application often have vague topics that can work with many different stories.

timed essays, like those on the SAT and ACT). Crafting a well-written personal essay begins with effective brainstorming.

It's important to take this step seriously. Don't be tempted to rush in or skip it. In many ways, brainstorming is the most important part of the writing process; without it, you're gambling with success. You could spend hours writing an eloquent piece that might get you an A in your English class, but doesn't work as a personal essay. Take the time to think about the story you want to tell. What do you want admissions counselors to know about you? What information will help them see you as more than a list of activities, grades, and test scores?

Find Your Voice and Find Your Story: Journaling

Here's a common piece of college essay writing advice: *your personal statement should be written in your own voice.* But what does that mean? You have a voice you use with your friends, another with your teachers, and still another with your parents. Which one is right for your essay? One of the easiest ways to find the right voice for your essay is to keep a journal.

This might seem like odd advice and unrelated to the major task you have to accomplish. But it is actually a great method for beginning your essay, for two important reasons. The first is that your journal will sound like you and allow you to practice honing your voice. Rachel Klein-Ash, a college counselor at Milton Academy in Milton, Massachusetts, advises her students to keep journals to help with essay writing because they can "give them back their own words." Journals, Klein-Ash says, are like "your mind coming out on paper." When you are writing your essay, you can use the journal as a reference for tone and word choices that convey your authentic voice.

The second reason for keeping a journal is that it can be a great source of ideas. In it, you can write about what's important to you, your goals and aspirations, your values, and your take on everything from popular culture to current events. Your journal, coupled with the information you gather in your inventory (which we'll get to later in this chapter), is the perfect source of raw data from which to begin the essay writing process.

Journaling doesn't have to be an elaborate, time-consuming process. Take as little as five minutes a day to write about something personal. In order to journal effectively you need to make it a routine, so the process needs to be as simple and painless as possible. Think about your daily habits and routine, and employ a journaling strategy that best suits you. You can write on paper, make journal entries on your computer, or keep a blog.

Pick a time and place to write in your journal each day. If you're writing on paper, get a journal that's small enough to carry with you everywhere you go. Therefore, when inspiration hits you'll be ready. If you're typing, set aside a specific time to work at your computer. To avoid distractions, open your journal document before going online and stick with it for the allotted time period.

If you're considering keeping an online journal or blog, visit www.my-diary.org, www.blogger.com, or www.livejournal.com to see how they're set up. Some sites require you to type entries while online, and others have downloadable diaries that can be added to at any time. A word of warning: the potential problem with these sites is the distractions. There are other diarist's entries to read, software to play around with, and features such as uploading pictures, all of which can keep you from your real task. If you're having trouble staying focused, choose the handwritten or simple word processing journal option.

When journaling in an effort to find admissions essay material, limit yourself to writing about your experiences, thoughts, and feelings. This could include your view of the world, a good or bad thing that happened to you each day, your school, and your friends and family. Remember to keep it focused on *you*. Use the following prompts to help you if you get stuck or need some direction.

INSIDER INFORMATION

"If you want your essay to stand out, think about what other students will choose to write about. Because of our location in Southern California, we see a lot of essays about volunteer trips to Mexico. They're pretty generic. Ask yourself if anyone else could have written your essay, and if the answer is yes, think about changing your topic. I'd like to get to know the individual student by reading something unique."

—JONATHAN GÓMEZ,
admissions counselor,
Loyola Marymount University

- **Write a letter to someone who has had a significant influence on you.** Use as many details and anecdotes as possible to *show*, rather than *tell*, why they are so important.
- **Choose a current event, and discuss its importance.** Be as personal as possible. How has the event changed your thinking? How does it make you feel? How has it impacted your daily life or future plans?
- **Describe a risk you took, and what you gained or lost by taking it.** Did you learn something about yourself or the world? Are you a different person because you took the risk? Was it worth it?
- **Choose a creative work that is of particular importance to you.** How has it influenced you? Describe it in great detail and remember to keep it personal.
- **Describe a travel experience that affected you somehow.** Recount the experience as specifically as possible, using all five senses to detail it.
- **Describe a ritual you perform often that has meaning to you.** It's ok to think small. Do you meditate while setting the table? Do you listen to a certain kind of music while studying or reading? Do you cook something for yourself when you're stressed out? Don't worry if the ritual is quirky or that it may not seem important to someone else.
- **Imagine a perfect world.** What does *perfect* mean to you? Get as detailed as possible. Aside from the requisite world peace and clean environment, think about the day-to-day things that would make a difference to you. Would every coffee maker have a pause and serve feature? Would your favorite band perform free concerts at your school every Saturday? Would everyone in your state, upon getting their driver's license, be given the car of their choice for free?

GREAT QUESTION!

"I keep hearing about anecdotes, but I'm not sure what it means. Describing something that happened to me could take hundreds of words before I even start talking about myself. How should I handle this?"

An anecdote is a *short* retelling of an event or experience. In your essay, anecdotes can be used as an effective introduction and add some personality to your writing.

INSIDER INFORMATION

Admissions officers value some qualities over others, and you don't need to look any further than the Common Application to find out what they are. The Teacher Recommendation form asks your instructors to rate you in the following areas:

- creative and original thought
- motivation
- self-confidence
- initiative
- independence
- intellectual promise
- academic achievement
- disciplined work habits
- quality of writing
- productive class discussion
- respect accorded by faculty
- maturity
- leadership
- integrity
- reaction to setbacks
- concern for others

What activities and experiences can you write about that highlight one or more of these? How can you show (rather than tell) in your essay that you have these qualities? Keep them in mind when filling out your inventory.

Once you begin the essay writing stage, your journal will become an invaluable tool for developing possible essay material. It can help you to choose the right tone, neither too casual nor too formal, so that your essay sounds like *you*. While reviewing your journal, make note of the words you use and what your voice sounds like. Also make note of the ideas and topics that hold your interest. Sometimes we're not aware of our feelings about something until we take the time to explore them.

Your Personal Inventory

The following inventory is designed to help you mine your life for material that you can use in your essay. It will also help you catalog possible subjects, and be useful when filling out the rest of your applications. Although you probably won't use all, or even most, of the information you gather, you should be willing to explore many possibilities before narrowing down your essay topic.

To complete your personal inventory, list everything that comes to mind for each section. Remember that brainstorming is not the time to censor yourself. Don't leave out something because you think it won't work. Be as non-judgmental as possible.

1. *History*

Think back to your earliest memory, and go from there. Move chronologically, cataloging events in your life until you reach the most recent one(s). Don't limit yourself to only dramatic or life-altering experiences. Spend the most time on the past few years; childhood memories rarely create a useful picture of who you are today. Use the following space to write down your ideas:

_____

_____

_____

_____

_____

_____

_____

_____

_____

_____

_____

_____

_____

_____

_____

_____

_____

2. Achievements and Accomplishments

List all awards or other commendations you have received (academic, extracurricular, etc.). Also include goals you have reached or accomplished that may not have been explicitly recognized by others. What milestones have been important to you and your personal growth? What achievements are you most proud of? Use the following space to write down your ideas:

3. Activities

Outside of the classroom, what have you spent your time doing? These may be one-time or ongoing activities. Keep the following areas in mind (but don't limit yourself to these): sports, civic groups, travel, volunteer work, art projects, technology, and religious groups. Why did you start the activity, and, if applicable, why do you continue with it? Remember, many of these may be listed in other places on your application. Think about things you've done that are not mentioned elsewhere, or have not been given significant attention on the rest of the application. Here is where you can expand. Use the following space to write down your ideas:

4. *Influences*

Make a list of the people, events, works of art, literature, and music that have affected you. Use the following space to write down your ideas:

_____

_____

_____

_____

_____

_____

_____

_____

_____

_____

_____

_____

_____

_____

_____

_____

_____

_____

_____

_____

5. Skills

What are you good at? You may want to ask friends and family members to help with this. Skills may be those acquired through learning and practice, such as playing an instrument, or may include personal attributes, such as leadership or willingness to follow the road not taken. Use the following space to write down your ideas:

_____

_____

_____

_____

_____

_____

_____

_____

_____

_____

_____

_____

_____

_____

6. Passions

What makes your blood boil or your heart beat faster? Is there a sports team you follow with fervor, a book you've read many times, a topic of local, national, or global importance that gets you riled up? You may have listed these in other sections, but repeat them here because this category examines them from a different point of view. Use the following space to write down your ideas:

7. Family

It might sound ordinary to you, but a story about a parent, sibling, or other relative can make a great essay. The more specific you get, the more unique this topic will become. Remember that colleges are looking for students who have the emotional maturity and stability to stay in school and excel—showing that you have a strong family base of support can do just that. Use the following space to write down your ideas:

_____

_____

_____

_____

_____

_____

_____

_____

_____

_____

_____

_____

_____

_____

_____

_____

Show, Don't Tell

A third brainstorming technique begins with friends and family. Ask at least three people to write a short list of adjectives that describe you. Collect the lists, and blend them to create a new one. Place any repeated words at the top of the new list.

Next, write a short essay based on your top three personal adjectives—and discuss them without using them. Instead, use anecdotes and experiences to describe yourself, to *show* the adjectives rather than *tell* them. This is a key distinction, and a change that can make a decent essay into one that really stands out. To make sure that your descriptions are solid, have a friend or family member read your essay and try to figure out what the adjectives were.

Right Brain Triggers

The following brainstorming exercise comes from Liz Leroux, a college essay consultant at Strategies for College. She advises students to make a *life map*. Begin by taping together a few sheets of blank paper. Then, using markers or crayons, draw stick figures and cartoon-like illustrations to represent moments from your life, starting at the bottom and working your way up the paper. According to Leroux:

> *"These images often trigger some great ideas. In a recent one I did for a seminar, I started with a picture of five blue stick figures and a little pink one. Above those, I drew a figure in a weeping willow tree. From those pictures I came up with an idea I hadn't thought of before: growing up as the only girl with five brothers, I climbed trees to find some space in my big family. In the quiet of the tree, I could create stories for my paper dolls and imagine I was a writer."*

As you create your life map, aim for about 10–12 images. This technique will force the left side of your brain (the part that's logical and objective) to work with the right side (the part that's intuitive and subjective). Many writers become blocked because the left brain edits ideas before they can be adequately explored. But here, you're creating images without deciding first if they'd work for an essay. The right brain's tendency to allow for all possibilities is free to work without being stifled. But the left and right brain don't just think differently. Memories

GREAT QUESTION!

"Show versus tell: what's the difference?"

The distinction between *showing* and *telling* is an important one, and it can make the difference between a boring essay and one that really stands out—even if both essays are written about the same subject. Think of *showing* as examples and illustrations that answer the question *How?* or *What do you mean?* When you're *telling*, you're making a statement that's not backed up. Here are some quick show versus tell statements:

Tell: I'm a really good piano player.
Show: I mastered Gershwin's *Preludes* for my senior recital.
Tell: My summer job at the grocery store taught me a lot about responsibility.
Show: After three weeks on the job, I was promoted to assistant produce manager, and I had to direct three other employees.
Tell: Traveling to Vietnam introduced me to another culture.
Show: Eating crickets in Hanoi, riding in a pedicab or *xich lo*, and bargaining for clothing in Hoi An were incredible experiences that showed me how differently people live.

are stored in the right brain, so an exercise that induces you to use that part of the brain can help you unlock things long forgotten. "You may be surprised by the results," Leroux adds.

Great Essays: Some Final Thoughts

While almost any experience can be the basis of a great essay, here's how to avoid committing common essay blunders:

- **Positive is probably better.** You could write a superb essay on the anxiety you've experienced as a teenager, or your struggle with depression, but think about your audience. How many times does an admissions officer want to read depressing topics?
- **Think recent past.** Essay readers want to know about who you are today, not about your early childhood. Unless it has significant relevance to who you are today, skip it.

- **Keep unflattering experiences to yourself.** You want to be liked. Don't write about major screw-ups or stupid things you did. You want to sound competent and responsible. Success out of failure stories only work if you focus on how you learned a great lesson and grew as a person. Stay positive as you describe turning an obstacle into an achievement. Sob stories or excuses must be avoided.

- **Avoid clichés.** Peace in the middle east, why my volunteer position helps me more than those I'm supposed to be helping, how my friend's death taught me to enjoy life more, teen angst—these have all been done many times before. Unless your take on a popular topic is highly original and personal, you run the risk of boring your audience. Showcase your uniqueness by steering clear of obvious topics and content.

- **Think local, not global.** Large societal or political issues are usually not personal. Global subjects, such as world peace, have been expounded upon by experts, and you probably don't have a unique perspective (unless you were personally involved or impacted). Think specific and personal rather than abstract and global.

- **Resist any temptation to brag.** Don't go overboard highlighting your achievements, and especially don't take credit for something you shouldn't. For example, did your team really win the state championship because of your leadership skills? There is a great difference between advocating for yourself and sounding pompous. Be careful.

3 SELECTING AND WORKING WITH A TOPIC

Admissions departments give great thought to the essay topics they include on their applications. They're designed to help you reveal something about yourself, and, in turn, to help them decide whom to accept. Chris Ajamian, CEO of Cates Tutoring, uses a *roommate theory* when helping students with their essays. "Look at the big picture," he stresses. "The purpose of the essay is to show colleges what kind of roommate you'll be. Who are you beyond the numbers, and what will you contribute to the community?"

Some essay topics have a different angle though. They're still personal, but are intended to disclose something called *demonstrated interest*. This is a relatively new concept in admissions essays, and its appearance coincided with the rise in the number of applications each school started receiving. Simply put, it's an attempt to gauge how enthusiastic you are about attending if you're accepted (since many students apply to seven or more schools, chances are they're only vaguely interested in some of them, and admissions officers would rather not bother with those who seem to have applied on a whim).

Many of these demonstrated interest topics are included in Common Application supplements (additional information required by some schools), and they also appear as prompts for required second short answer essays. While they vary from one application to another, these topics typically fall into one of two categories: asking you why you're applying, or getting you to connect with a specific issue of interest to the school.

In the last chapter, you learned how to develop a unique story or stories suitable for your admissions essay. In this chapter we'll explore the types of topics that appear on most applications. Although you're often able to write on any subject (many schools offer a version of "topic of your choice"), sometimes the parameters are much narrower, especially for supplemental essays. Whether you're choosing a topic or responding to a required one, it's important to first understand what each one is really asking for, and how best to approach it. If you've got a choice, this information can also help you determine which topic will best represent you on your application.

Common Application Topics

The Common Application, which is accepted by almost 400 colleges and universities across America, offers six essay topics. Since many other schools use similar prompts, it makes sense to begin with them. Each topic is explained with an emphasis on best approaches, what admissions officers are looking for, and what to avoid.

1. **Evaluate a significant experience, achievement, risk you have taken, or ethical dilemma you have faced, and its impact on you.** *The last phrase is critical—whatever you choose to write about (the cause), you must show its impact upon you (the effect). Your experience need not be earth shattering; keeping it small can often work better. Remember, you are guaranteed to write a unique essay if you focus on something that you alone experienced or find meaning in.*

ADVICE FROM THE PROS

"Common Application topics? They're helpful for students who really can't decide what to write about. It gives them a place to start. But don't just answer a question. Go off and tell a story about yourself."

—CHRIS AJEMIAN, CEO, CATES Tutoring

For example, writing an essay on what it felt like to drive a car alone for the first time, or why you enjoy preparing a favorite recipe, can showcase your creativity and ability to make connections with something larger than yourself. Perhaps the cooking experience showed you how a bunch of little steps can add up to something big, or how a simple recipe can connect you with your ethnic heritage.

In other words, they don't want to know about how you took first prize in the Mozart piano competition. If you want to write about piano playing, you could briefly mention the prize, but focus on explaining how the rigors of practice, the wisdom of your teacher, and the knowledge of musical composition have changed you for the better.

2. **Discuss some issue of personal, local, national, or international concern and its importance to you.** *Be careful here, many experts caution against writing on this topic unless the issue has had a profound and highly personal effect on you. It lends itself to clichés (i.e. why I want world peace) and can steer you away from your task, which is to reveal something about yourself.*

   Another potential problem with this topic is that you can alienate yourself from your reader. You don't know who your essay will be read by, so be careful not to dismiss or critique the other side of your argument while laying out your own.

   Since this topic is not among the most popular (fewer than five percent of students choose it), you'll stand out simply by writing on it. But here's the balance you'll need to find—display your knowledge of the issue while keeping the focus highly personal.

3. **Indicate a person who has had a significant influence on you, and describe that influence.** *At first thought, this topic looks like an easy way to write a unique essay. You might be thinking, "How many students were influenced by Mother Theresa the way I've been?" You'd be surprised. It's difficult to choose a famous person who hasn't already been the subject of thousands of admissions essays. And second on the list of overdone* person of influence *essays is relatives (parents and grandparents are the overwhelming favorites), followed closely by coaches.*

   If you do choose this topic, be fully aware of the cliché potential. Here's your focus—get highly creative in your explanation of how he or she influenced you. Be careful though, this can lead to more cliché possibilities. How unique is your parent's guidance or your coach's leadership abilities? No matter who you write about, remember that the question is a catalyst for revealing information about you, not about your person of influence. Don't simply describe the person. Show evidence of yourself throughout your essay by relating everything back to you.

INSIDER INFORMATION

"Students who tell me nothing about themselves are making the biggest essay mistake. Even if it's very well written, an essay that isn't personal doesn't work."

—JONATHAN GÓMEZ,
admissions counselor,
Loyola Marymount University

ONLINE ESSAY PRACTICE

Although it's called the personal essay, many students still write hundreds of words about anything and everything but themselves. When this happens, the opportunity to make a connection with the reader and stand out, is lost.

In this online exercise, you'll be able to respond to a prompt, and then get a score based on five key essay elements: **organization**, **support**, **sentence structure**, **grammar/word choice**, and **mechanics**. The feedback will help you uncover your strengths and weaknesses as a writer. But more important for this exercise is your ability to turn the prompt into a vehicle through which you can express something about yourself.

To complete this online activity, go to the **Additional Online Practice** page on page 131 and follow the instructions.

Once you have logged in, click **Start** under the prompt titled *Expository Essay: Courageous Character.*

Here's the prompt:

Filmmaker Orson Welles once said that courage is the most important human virtue. Think of a character from a novel, play, poem, or film, or a real person in history who you feel acted courageously. Now, write to describe how that character or person displayed courage.

For this exercise, add the following:

Don't stop with the character or person. In fact, use only a few sentences to respond to that portion of the prompt. Continue by explaining how that character's courage has influenced you. Put the emphasis on what you've learned, or how you've been changed.

Click in the empty white box under the instructions and begin to type your sample essay response to this prompt. Periodically click **Save** to make sure that your work is not erased! When you are finished writing your essay, click **Next Page**. If you'd like to review your work before having it scored, click **Back**. If you are happy with your essay and feel it is complete, click **Score My Test**.

You will receive an automatic essay score from 1–6, evaluating you on the five elements discussed above. Click on the link titled **View Scoring Guide** to get a better sense of the criteria used to evaluate your essay. In addition to getting a sense of the mechanical aspects of your essay, take another look at what you have written by clicking on **View Essay**.

After you have reread what you've written, ask yourself:

- What does the reader now know about me?
- Could I have revealed this information anywhere else on my application? (the fact that you're a soccer player, student government president, or youth group member, for example, is easily listed under extracurricular activities)
- Could anyone else have written this essay?
- Will my essay help the reader understand why I should be accepted?

4. **Describe a character in fiction, a historical figure, or a creative work (as in art, music, science, etc.) that has had an influence on you, and explain that influence.** *This is the least popular Common Application topic—and for good reason. As with choice number three, you need to keep the focus on you, not the character or creative work. That's not easy to do, especially if you choose an obscure character or work that can't be explained in a short paragraph. Your choice of topic does disclose something about you, but you need to reveal even more by showing how she/he/it has influenced you. Remember to stay on task.*

The best way to approach this topic is to choose someone or something that the reader has probably heard of; too much description or background information is a waste of words that should be used to write about yourself. However, you also want to be original, so think about the choices other students will probably make, especially when it comes to historical figures. The more obvious the hero type, the more likely students have written about him or her.

Another potential problem with the choice of a subject is the possibility of being offensive. While it's good to be unique, it's also important to be appropriate. You don't want to put off your reader or give the impression that you aren't taking the essay seriously. Writing about an anti-hero (think Idi Amin or Charles Manson) or a foolish or rude character is not a smart gamble. There are two things you know definitively about your reader: he or she is older than you and gainfully employed in higher education. Anticipate that this reader may not share your sense of humor or taste.

Once you've chosen an appropriate subject that is neither too obscure nor too popular or offensive, zero in on the last three words of the prompt: *explain that influence.* If at least two-thirds of your essay isn't explaining, you've missed the point of this topic. Your focus must be on you, rather than on the character or work of art.

INSIDER INFORMATION

Ever wonder why only about 25 percent of schools use the Common Application? The Common Application Association is committed to a holistic admissions process. This means that its member schools evaluate candidates not simply on their grades and test scores, but also on less numerical factors, such as the essay and teacher evaluations.

HERE'S WHAT WORKED

"The goal is to reveal something about you, but there is also some vagueness about the boundaries or limits. It's important to be bold—don't be afraid to show who you are—but at the same time you need to think about what not to share. Strike a balance between being revealing and being appropriate."

—MATTHEW FISHMAN,
college freshman

5. **A range of academic interests, personal perspectives, and life experiences adds much to the educational mix. Given your personal background, describe an experience that illustrates what you would bring to the diversity of a college community, or an encounter that has demonstrated the importance of diversity to you.** *Diversity is a key word in admissions today. While admissions offices have always sought to create classes in which there is a wide range of abilities, viewpoints, and backgrounds (imagine if every freshman was a leader, or a gymnast, or a drummer), in recent years, schools are even more eager to tout the diversity of their student body. Just try finding a school website that doesn't feature pictures of different students engaged in a range of activities, along with a demographic breakdown showing the states, countries, races, and ethnicities those students represent.*

That said, this topic is the most recent addition to the Common Application list, and many schools use something similar. (Notre Dame's is: "The Rev. John I. Jenkins, C.S.C., President of the University of Notre Dame, said in his Inaugural Address that, 'If we are afraid to be different from the world, how can we make a difference in the world?' In what way do you feel you are different from your peers, and how will this shape your contribution to the Notre Dame community?") Notre Dame's prompt is a good one to keep in mind because it makes clear the fact that diversity is not just about race. Think of diversity not as a politically correct code word, but as another way to express uniqueness.

If you choose this topic, you'll need to focus on a viewpoint, an interest, a passion, a pastime—something about you that makes you stand out. And as with every essay, the focus should stay on *you*. That said, there are two major potential pitfalls: being generic and being offensive. The first recalls advice from admissions counselor Jonathan Gómez of Loyola Marymount University: describing the volunteer trip to a third world country (or New Orleans, Appalachia, or Mexico) can be clichéd. Many students have taken trips like this, and your revelation may sound very familiar. "I learned that I don't need much to be happy," "I am much more privileged than I thought I was," or "Poverty will never mean the same thing to me;" while these are all well-intentioned observations, they're not unique—and they can easily move from clichéd to offensive, which is the second major pitfall.

As described in chapter 1, admissions officers are themselves diverse. You don't know your reader. Descriptions can easily veer into the distasteful, without your even being aware of it. What one person thinks is an acceptable description can easily be read by another as stereotyping. Remember that the focus of the essay is on you, and the element(s) of diversity you will bring to campus. Using your essay to describe an encounter with diversity, whether through an acquaintance or on a journey, can easily divert your essay from its purpose and potentially offend your reader.

6. **Topic of your choice.** *This question is found on many applications in various forms. One school asks "We want to get to know you as a person. Make up a question that is personally relevant to you, state it clearly, and answer it. Feel free to use your imagination, recognizing that those who read it will not mind being entertained." Another puts it this way: "The application lists several topic suggestions, but feel free to write about any subject that you feel is relevant and will enable us to get to know you."*

Any personal story, such as the one(s) you uncovered in chapter 2, will obviously work with this topic, so it's not surprising that about 40 percent of students who submit the Common Application choose it. However, as with the request for a writing sample, this topic also lends itself to essay recycling. If you already have a well-written, vivid piece on something of great significance to you, something you know well, and that has changed or had a great impact on you, you may use it here.

INSIDER INFORMATION

Want to stand out simply by responding to an essay topic most students avoid? Here's the latest breakdown for Common Application topics:

- Topic 1 (significant experience): 6.44%
- Topic 2 (issue of importance): 4.55%
- Topic 3 (person of influence): 14.82%
- Topic 4 (character or historical figure): 3.20%
- Topic 5 (ethical dilemma): 31.70%
- Topic 6 (topic of choice): 39.29%

Demonstrated Interest Topics

The term *demonstrated interest* describes a student's efforts in showing that a school is at the top of his or her list. Admissions officers gauge this interest in an attempt to predict who will attend if admitted. It's not surprising to learn that they would rather admit students who are actually planning to put down a deposit if they get in. Many schools even track how many times students make contact, including visits, phone calls, e-mails, website registrations, and college fair meetings. If they don't they may ask you on their application to give the number and dates of contacts you've made.

Some schools use direct essay prompts that are intended to help determine how eager you are to attend their school, and what your contribution to their community will be. These prompts fall into two general types: those that ask why you're applying, either directly or indirectly, and those that prompt you to explain how you'll fit in. With these outcomes in mind, it's important to also consider the challenges common to demonstrated interest topics.

1. **Why are you applying to our school?**
    This topic appears in many forms, including:
    -   "Why Clark?"
    -   "What factors have led you to consider Macalester College? Why do you believe it may be a good match, and what do you believe you can add to the Mac community, academically and personally? Feel free to draw on past experiences, and use concrete examples to support your perspective. Additional writing samples (e.g., class papers or creative writing) are welcomed as supplements, but are not substitutes for either essay."
    -   "How did you first become interested in Reed, and why do you think Reed would be an appropriate place, both academically and socially, to continue your education? (This essay is instrumental in helping the admission committee determine the match between you and Reed, so be thorough.)"

        What they want to hear: that you will attend if they accept you, that you will graduate from their school, and that you have something meaningful to contribute to the school community.

        This topic typically requires research using resources beyond the school website and other material published by the school. Are there alumni or current students in your area? Talk to them about what the school is really like, and use this material to highlight your unique personality. Does the school host an international science fair every year? Mention it if you are dying to meet and speak with a renowned scientist who frequently attends. Does the literary magazine win top honors at the national level? Include some of your poetry and write about your dream of getting published and working in the publishing industry.

2. Are you a good fit for our community?

Some schools are looking for particular qualities in their applicants, either because they have a strong sense of mission or they've decided to embrace something specific, such as study abroad or volunteerism, and want to admit students who will willingly participate. But this topic typically won't be worded quite as directly as the question above. Instead, you'll find prompts such as this example from Loyola Marymount University:

Statement: A motto often associated with Jesuit and Marymount schools is "Educating men and women for others." Fr. Pedro Arrupe, the former head of the Jesuits, once said that "our prime educational objective must be to form men and women for others, who believe that a love of self or of God which does not issue forth in justice for the least of their neighbors is a farce."

Question: What do you think Fr. Arrupe meant when he said this? Please give an example of someone you know, other than your teachers and parents, who works for justice for the least of their neighbors.

The following prompt asks students to explain themselves and their goals in terms of the school's values: "Pitzer College was founded in 1963, the same year Martin Luther King, Jr. gave his famous 'I Have A Dream' speech, which had a fundamental impact upon our nation and the world. Reflecting on Pitzer's core values (intercultural understanding, social responsibility, interdisciplinary emphasis, and student autonomy), what is your dream for your time at Pitzer and how will that influence you to make a positive impact?"

When faced with such a prompt, it's important to think about your fit with the school. If you can relate to the topic, and it doesn't take much brainstorming to come up with good essay content, then you're probably making a good choice. Conversely, if the topic seems challenging and you're at a loss for ideas, you might want to reconsider applying. These types of prompts are designed to weed out those who won't fit in—and it's much easier (not to mention cheaper) for you to make that decision before you submit your application.

Note the strong similarities between these prompts and some of those found on the Common Application. While their intention is slightly more complex (schools are interested in finding out exactly how much you want to be a part of their community), they're still prompting personal responses. Don't miss the opportunity to share something about yourself that isn't evident on the rest of your application, and to make a connection with your reader.

While the Loyola topic asks you to give an example of someone you know who works for justice, remember the essay's true purpose. Mention that person's good works, but relate it to your life. Do you plan to do similar work? Why or why not? Also be sure to keep the focus on the values discussed—writing an essay that skims over or belittles what are obviously deeply held beliefs won't work here.

Demonstrating Interest without a Prompt

Admissions counselors rank demonstrated interest as a decision factor that's gaining in importance. Even if you don't get a specific prompt, you can use the Common Application's topic of your choice to write an essay that reveals how interested you are in attending a particular school. If this is your plan, it's critical that you do your homework.

> "Admissions officers are usually very skilled at reading students, so do not think of this process as a game and try to fake your interest."
>
> —MARILYN EMERSON,
> college counselor

Here are a couple of ideas:

- **Research your intended major.** If you're applying to a school that has achieved recognition for that major, or if your major is a rare one and only a few schools offer it, you've got a good place to start. For example, there are only a few dozen schools that offer a major in agribusiness. Check the courses offered through your major's department, as well as the list of professors who teach them. On many sites, the professor's recent publications, research, and specific areas of interest will be listed. What appeals to you? Why do you want to study with one or more of these professors? Are there research opportunities you would like to get involved in? These are the kinds of details that can show how interested you are in attending.

ADVICE FROM THE PROS

- **Visit the college.** This investment in time (and often expense if the location is far from home) demonstrates a sincere interest. While there, take the tour, sit in on a class, and talk with students. If you're interested in majoring in a specific department, arrange to meet with a professor or students in that department and ask questions.
- **Request an on-campus interview.** Take advantage of this option if the college offers it, or try to meet with an alumnus in your area. Prepare for the interview by learning about the school and thinking about what you want the interviewer to know about you. This request shows initiative on your part.
- **Arrange to visit with a representative at a local or national college fair.** If you cannot visit a school, you can see if there are any upcoming college fairs in your area at the National Association for College Admissions Counseling website, www.nacacnet.org.
- **Identify the Regional Admissions Officer at each college on your list.** This is the person responsible for admissions applications from your part of the country. Get to know this person, both through e-mail and phone conversations. Ask this person to help you decide if the school is a good fit for you.
- **Spend time on the college's website.** Stay on top of school news and happenings. Colleges keep track of how often you contact them and visit their site.
- **Respond promptly to recruiting e-mails or correspondence.**
- **Meet with the admissions officer if he or she is visiting your high school or local area.**
- **Develop a relationship with someone at the college or university.**
- **Let the college know if it is your first choice or a top choice.**
- **Attend a prospective student day.**
- **Participate in online chats.**

- **Check mission statements.** Grinnell College, for example, states in part that it "aims to graduate women and men who can think clearly, who can speak and write persuasively and even eloquently, who can evaluate critically both their own and others' ideas, who can acquire new knowledge, and who are prepared in life and work to use their knowledge and their abilities to serve the common good." Students who are compelled to work to serve the common good could write about how their goals mesh with those of the university.

Quotation Prompts

Many schools use quotations, both famous and obscure, as essay topics. While some provide a specific question to help direct your writing, others simply ask you to respond in any way you choose. For example, Amherst College does the latter, citing three separate quotes to choose from. One of them is the following:

> *"It seems to me incumbent upon this and other schools' graduates to recognize their responsibility to the public interest...unless the graduates of this college... are willing to put back into our society those talents, the broad sympathy, the understanding, the compassion...then obviously the presuppositions upon which our democracy are based are bound to be fallible."*

> —JOHN F. KENNEDY, at the ground breaking
> for the Amherst College Frost Library,
> October 26, 1963

Not all schools use heavyweight quotes. George Washington University, for example, provides:

> *"A table, a chair, a bowl of fruit and a violin; what else does a man need to be happy?"*

> —A. EINSTEIN

The directions provided by Amherst College are great advice, no matter the quotation or the school: "It is not necessary to research, read, or refer to the texts from which these quotations are taken; we are looking for original, personal responses to these short excerpts. Remember that your essay should be personal in nature and not simply an argumentative essay."

Short Answer Prompts

Some schools ask you to write more than one essay in an attempt to elicit additional information about you. Second and even third essays are typically expected to be 250 words or fewer, and their topics are often wide-ranging. As with every essay, resist the temptation to get scholarly—these aren't meant to demonstrate your research or debate skills.

Here are a few other examples:

- **University of Richmond:** Tell us about an experience in which you left your comfort zone. How did this experience change you?
- **Stetson University:** If you had a million dollars today, what would you do with it?
- **University of Virginia:** What is your favorite word and why?

Recycling Essays

Many prompt types lend themselves to essay recycling; consider the timesaving move of using an essay you've already written. Here are three ideas for making the most of existing essays:

1. **Submit the original copy of an essay you wrote for a class, with teacher comments.** Be certain to use an essay that got you an A and is on an interesting topic. There is an important advantage of this choice (other than the obvious saving of time and effort): it effectively gives you another teacher recommendation if the comments are positive and he or she didn't already write one of your other recommendations.

2. **Rewrite an essay composed for a class, improving it by incorporating teacher comments.** This option allows you to take advantage of your teacher's editing abilities. There is no need to mention the grade the essay received, or the class or teacher it was required by.

3. **Use an essay written for another college application.** If you use this option, just be sure your essay isn't geared specifically for another school. Carefully check the essay for any reference to a particular school before submitting it; more than one student has been caught extolling the virtues of school A on the application for school B. There's never an excuse for such sloppiness.

Making the Choice

Now that you're familiar with essay topics, you'll need to make a decision. If you came up with a great story in chapter 3, and you're using the Common Application, you'll simply need to choose topic 6 and move on to chapter 4. Otherwise, the following steps will help you select a prompt that best works with the information you'd like to share:

1. For each potential topic, use a separate sheet of paper and write it at the top.

2. Write anything that comes to mind in response to that topic. Your ideas can be in the form of a neat list, moving from most to least important, or they can be random.

3. Get out your personal inventory, and match information with the topics. Does your experience and background fit well with a particular topic? What about your creative interest? It could be narrowed down to a specific creative work or body of work (topic 4), or work well as a significant life experience (topic 1) if you write about your visit to New York to attend a seminar at the Fashion Institute of Technology.

Once you have prewriting notes on each topic, answer the following:

- Can I answer the question or address the topic completely?
- Does the topic let me highlight something about myself that wasn't evident on the rest of the application?
- Is the topic about something personally significant and important to my life?
- Can I make the essay unique, easily avoiding clichés?
- Will my essay on this topic tell the committee something they will like about me?
- Can I write about this topic without bragging or overstating my importance?
- Will my essay hold the interest of the reader?
- Will my essay avoid potentially offensive subjects?

Still Not Sure?

At this point, it may be clear which topic best suits your strengths and experiences, lending itself to a unique and insightful essay. However, if more than one topic seems like a good fit, here's another idea to help you make a choice. Go back to your personal inventory. Using a different colored highlighter for each topic, mark the information that could be used to write on that topic. To which topic can you bring the most actual experiences and concrete details? Still not sure? Consider outlining and writing rough drafts of two essays.

One student used a couple of Common Application topics to brainstorm two essays. She knew the information she wanted to share in the essay, but wasn't sure where she wanted to go with it. The prompts gave her some direction and helped her to craft an effective final essay, an excerpt of which follows:

"After I wrote the first one, I reread it, and realized that I had told a memory of something I really liked, but nothing more. Rather than trying to fix it, I simply began again. I wrote another essay a few days later, and a similar thing occurred. After reading it, I just didn't feel a click. This happened until my fourth essay. Although I only had a rough draft, I knew I had hit upon something good. I felt the click. It just worked better than the other topics."

—LIZ ABERNATHEY,
high school senior

Indicate a person who has had a significant influence on you, and describe that influence.

When my science teacher assigned a research paper on a scientist of our choice, I wasn't thrilled. I had no one in mind for the month-long project. I sat at the keyboard in the school library, looking for inspiration. Finally, I started a search for women scientists. I found a hit with a quote from Al Gore, calling the mystery person "an outstanding role model for women scientists across America."

Who was she? The late Dr. Nancy Foster, former Assistant Administrator for Oceanic Services and Coastal Zone Management at the National Oceanic and Atmospheric Administration, and Director of the National Ocean Service. The more I read about this brilliant, dynamic woman, the more I became inspired. Not only did I feel impressed and proud of her many accomplishments, but her story made me think that I could take my love of the ocean and its creatures and make it into a career as a marine biologist.

CHAPTER

4 THE WRITING PROCESS

With fewer than five minutes to make an impression on the reader, application essays must stand out—quickly. Once you've got a topic and subject, it's important to get your ideas in order, and gather the details that will get attention. By focusing, organizing, and detailing, you'll be able to present your story effectively and uniquely. Then you can turn your attention to using each part of the essay—introduction, body, and conclusion—to further enhance it.

Narrow Your Focus

Two of the most common problems with application essays are that they tend to be similar and hard to follow. Almost everyone who's writing an essay is the same age and have had many of the same experiences. Even if the story is unique, over-arching themes and descriptions used by high school students are fairly common. And when those students try to cover too much in the essay, it becomes hard to follow. But both of these problems can be remedied with one technique: *focus*.

In this context, focus means having a clear vision of what will be covered, and making sure the material is the right length for an admissions essay. With focus, you won't try to explain too much, skimming the surface and jumping from point to point because there isn't room for more thoughtful consideration. Think of focus as a very strong magnifying lens that enlarges just a key part of a long story. When you zero in on such a limited section, you can delve into it more deeply, exploring details and adding descriptions that enliven it.

Using that lens also raises your chances of being unique. For example, thousands of high school students play soccer. Most of them have played on winning teams—and losing ones. Their experiences with the sport are bound to be very similar. But, take a magnifying lens to one game, and then to one aspect of your participation in one game, and you're getting to the personal instead of the universal.

Try the lens in terms of piano lessons. Narrow the focus: the types of pieces you play? Maybe. Your teacher as a great influence? Probably done many times. Helping you overcome your fears? Good! Whether it's stage fright or the intense learning curve involved in mastering a piece, the fears associated with the instrument are a personal angle on a common theme. Notice that by focusing the topic, two things happen: it becomes more interesting, and it stands out because it's less generic. In addition, that magnifying lens is also helping to frame a story that can be covered well within the size limitations of the application essay.

> ## ADVICE FROM THE PROS
>
> *"It's important for every essay to cover something small—as small as possible. Think about how to condense your material into a day, an hour, or even a minute. This will give the reader something to focus on."*
>
> —LIZ LEROUX,
> former high school English teacher
> and college essay consultant

Plan First, Write Second

Many writers view outlines just as they view the brainstorming process—as a waste of time. Why not simply jump into a first draft? Here are a couple of reasons why you shouldn't: this is a high stakes assignment; in fact, it's probably the most important essay you'll write in high school. An outline not only gives you a plan to follow, but the act of creating one can help you organize and clarify your thoughts. It makes clear which points you want to make, and how they relate to and follow one another.

An outline can also help you build anticipation, grab attention, and make a better impression. Just changing the order of paragraphs and adding a few transitional sentences can heighten the momentum of an essay. Still not convinced? An outline will help you maintain focus by using the magnifying lens.

With an effective outline you won't veer off course, miss important points, or go off topic.

Creating an Essay Outline

Creating an outline begins with a reading of your inventory and prewriting notes. First, group related ideas together, looking for major topics (which can be headings), and minor ones (which can be subheadings, examples, or details). Define your major points, and rearrange them until they make sense and follow a logical progression. You'll be able to see the relationships between your ideas as you outline them and determine their importance (major point, minor point, example, detail). If you need more supporting details or facts—subcategories—you can add them here.

Standard Outline

If it has been a while since you've written one, a standard outline uses Roman and Arabic numerals and upper and lower case letters, as in the following sample outline.

This writer decided to organize her story chronologically, using physical places or objects (the bus, the camp, her home) to divide her story and to ground her emotional content. The complete essay is included in chapter 8.

I. Drive to regional soccer camp
- A. nervous about not being good enough
- B. weather makes nine-hour ride difficult
- C. find out grandma has had second stroke and is in hospital
  - 1. challenge is more emotional than physical

II. At camp
- A. not playing well; on reserve team
- B. phone calls from mom usually cheer me up
- C. mom tells me grandma is in a coma
  - 1. thinking about grandma is overwhelming
- D. while on field, see whole family approaching
- E. realize grandma has died

III. Home for the funeral
- A. comfort my aunt after the service
  - 1. realize I am support for her
- B. lucky to have my immediate family, unlike my aunt
- C. don't have the right words to say to her

IV. *Return to camp*
   A. *grandma would have wanted me to finish what I started*
      1. *feel obligated to follow through and take last chance to get chosen*
      2. *play in last game, on advanced team*
   B. *I am not selected*
V. *Return home*
   A. *see that some good can come out of situation*
      1. *able to help my aunt*
      2. *overcome my own grief*
      3. *have desire to continue to try to succeed*

Once you've completed your outline, revise and refine it by taking the following steps:

- **Write down your overall goal for your essay.** What are you trying to tell the admissions committee about yourself that the rest of your application didn't reveal?
- **Read through your outline.** While reading, circle, underline, or highlight your major points or images. Do they all support your goal?
- **Consider your focus.** Can your story be well told in about 500 words or are you trying to cover too much? Now is the time to get even narrower if need be.
- **Brainstorm details.** Include thoughts that will accurately and concisely express your major points. Write them down in the margin of your outline, or use a separate sheet.
- **Use your outline to guide your writing.** Don't allow yourself to stray from your goal, or your major points.

Add Depth with Details

The best way to make your essay stand out, and make your points clearly and vividly, is to use details. Remember back in chapter 2 when we discussed the difference between showing and telling? Details are a great way to show. They're also important because they help the reader connect with your writing—an important goal of your admissions essay.

Details often involve the senses. You might describe a scene or an object with such clarity that your reader can almost see it for him or herself. Also, use dialogue or sounds to help your reader connect with your essay. This is important in almost any kind of writing, but it is crucial in the personal essay. It's these kinds of details that express your unique experiences and point of view. In other words, details can turn a weak essay into a winner.

If you haven't started writing yet, think about details as you develop your notes and outline. For every point you make, come up with three or four details that support it. Get as specific as possible. Notice the impact additional details can have in the following descriptions:

- *We lived in a house.*
- *We lived in a typical center-hall colonial.*
- *We lived in a typical middle-class, subdivision house—the center hall colonial.*

Details also includes *instances* and *examples*. Don't tell your reader that you love the works of Jane Austen. Instead, show it by describing where and when you bought your first copy of *Emma*, or how you missed soccer practice because you were caught up reading *Pride and Prejudice* and forgot the time. Scenarios that illustrate your point can be great essay details. Take your reader to your jazz band performance by setting the scene. Describe the festival stage, the crowd, even the weather.

Specific evidence, such as the exact temperature of the ocean, or how many volunteers you were up against when you won the Volunteer of the Year award, are also strong details. By being precise, you draw your reader into further identification with your writing. And since your goal is to submit an essay that connects with at least one person on the admissions committee, that identification is critical.

Dialogue also makes for great essay detail. Giving strong voices to the people you're writing about makes them seem more real, and your interaction with them provides a glimpse into your ability to form relationships and get along with others. (Remember the *roommate theory* of personal essays? You're convincing your reader that you can live in one room with another student harmoniously.)

ADVICE FROM THE PROS

"Don't get so caught up in descriptions that you spend too much time writing about everything but your primary subject: you. The most important question to ask once you've got a draft is, could anyone else have written this essay? If the answer is yes, it's because there is not enough 'you' in it. Go back and focus in tighter. Details and descriptions are important, but they can distract you and take your essay away from its intended purpose."

—SUSAN GOODKIN,
Executive Director,
California Learning Strategies Center

HERE'S WHAT WORKED

"When my English teacher read my essay, he pointed out that I used too many adjectives. 'Six colors to describe one sunset? Maybe it's accurate, but it's boring. You're losing me,' he said. His advice was to describe with strong verbs instead of so many adjectives. I've never forgotten that advice, and I know it has made my writing much better."

—Sophomore history major, Ohio State University

One word of caution: be certain the details you use are related to your message and are not overdone. Whether it's a scenario, a description, or lines of dialogue, have a good reason for its inclusion. Don't leave it up to your reader to draw conclusions or figure out connections. Make certain each detail supports your major points and overall essay goals. And don't overdo it. Some admissions essays are clogged with details; perhaps it's because some students are used to writing assignments that are required to be a certain length, or because they've been taught that there's no such thing as too much description. It's important to strike a balance by using enough details to enliven your writing, but not so much that they weigh things down.

Vague and Detailed Sentences

Adding a few details can make boring sentences come alive. Note how the following details can express a unique personality and point of view.

Before: *I spent the summer working at Wal-Mart.*
After: *Eight hours a day, five days a week, I worked at Wal-Mart last summer, dreaming of the sun that would be setting as I punched out.*

Before: *Math is my favorite subject.*
After: *Calculus made me think in ways I never had before, and made me realize that I wanted to follow a career path that involves mathematics.*

Before: *I really want to attend XYZ University.*
After: *The two most important reasons for my decision to apply to XYZ University are its relationship to its inner city community, and the quality of the teaching staff in the Economics Department.*

Before: *Playing varsity baseball has taught me how to be part of a team.*
After: *I learned many valuable lessons from my teammates during my three years playing varsity baseball.*

Great Starts: The Introduction

Imagine a stack of 700 essays. Then imagine that it's your job to read and evaluate each one—in addition to your other professional duties. You can expect an admissions officer to spend about four minutes per essay, and that's if the first paragraph a) doesn't give away the content of the entire essay; b) isn't so poorly written that it's a tip-off that the student may not be ready for college-level writing; or c) isn't boring. While many in admissions read each and every essay from the first word to the last, others don't. That's why it's critical that your introduction be designed to entice. There are a number of effective ways to hook your reader from the opening sentences. Here are some great ways to create a hook:

- **Get emotional.** Your reader will relate to your subject if you engage their emotions and cause them to make a connection with you and your writing. Think about beginning your essay by discussing the way you felt about something, rather than first describing or otherwise revealing that something.
- **Be intriguing.** Your introduction needs to relate to the rest of your essay, but it can be a small detail that makes the admissions officers wonder what you are up to. Writing about how your music teacher has influenced you? You might begin by describing how his playing the cello makes you feel in a few detailed sentences. Don't mention that he is your teacher, or that he has helped shaped your love of music—yet. The reader will wonder who the mystery teacher is, and want to read more to find out.
- **Give an anecdote.** A very short *slice of life* story that doesn't clue the reader in to where you are headed can be a great hook. Write about the last seconds of a basketball game, checking out your last customer of the day, or your brilliant but disorganized teacher's lecture on Emerson. Admissions officers will have to keep reading to discover what you are writing about.
- **Ask a question.** *Have you ever heard of a basketball coach reading poetry to her team? Why would I want to give up my poolside summer as a lifeguard to work in a rundown, unairconditioned school?* Take your subject, and ask yourself what is unusual or in need of an explanation. Turn it into a question that doesn't have an obvious answer.
- **Cite an unusual fact.** Telling your reader something he or she doesn't know, and wouldn't guess, can compel him or her to read on. If you're writing about a travel experience, hunt down some statistics that might seem startling, like: *The U.S. Department of Transportation reported that*

during the month I was traveling, over 255,000 pieces of luggage were lost. Did your church youth group volunteer with migrant farm workers picking oranges? A few minutes of research can help you begin your essay: *Florida's Valencia orange forecast for April was 86 million boxes.*

Introductions That Hook Readers

Example:

I will never forget the moment I landed in Rio de Janeiro, Brazil. As the plane descended, I was awed by the dynamic geography and the juxtaposition of the sea, the mountains, and the city's skyline. I absorbed the landscape further and my eyes focused on the favelas mounted on the hillsides.

Why it works:

This introduction takes the reader to an exotic location, describes the landscape, and sets the scene. She tells you the moment is unforgettable, and brings you along with her. More importantly, she does not reveal anything about her subject. You have to read on to find out what her essay is about.

Example:

My thoughts were scattered. I couldn't concentrate on the directions I was being given, and my anxiety about taking the test only increased as I realized I needed to be paying attention. The more I told myself to relax, the worse it got. Palms sweating, heart beating wildly, I somehow got my gear on and jumped into the pool.

Why it works:

Who hasn't felt anxiety before a test? Using emotion as a hook works here not only because anyone can relate to those feelings, but also because the reader has no idea what kind of test is being taken. The mention of the pool gives some information without revealing the entire subject.

Example:

Tom Wessels slaps his felt hat over his bushy hair, and starts striding away with the confident gait of a hiker. The gritty March snow stings our eyes as we scramble to keep up with him, this master of the woods, wise man of the hills. His book, Reading the Forested Landscape, has been our bible at the Mountain School, an eternal reference to the woods. Few people get to meet the authors of books they read, so we speak to him with special reverence.

Why it works:

The reader gets to meet Tom Wessels in a well-written description of both the author and the setting in which the writer meets him. There is no indication where the essay is headed—it could be about Mr. Wessels as an influence, or about his book. In fact, it is really about the writer's love of the natural world, and how it was enhanced by her studies at the Mountain School, and *Reading the Forested Landscape.*

GREAT QUESTION!

"I'm stuck on my introduction. I know how important it is, but I can't seem to come up with something that stands out. What should I do?"

Here's the most important rule for introductions: wait to write it until after you've completed the rough draft of the rest of your essay. Then, extract something from your writing to use as a great opener.

The Meat of the Essay: Effective and Organized Body Paragraphs

The body of your essay should be the easiest part to write. Using your outline and notes, put down your thoughts in clear sentences that flow logically from one to another. As you write your rough draft, don't sweat every word. Later on, you'll be editing and getting feedback from other readers. However, if you find weaknesses with your outline as you write, such as missing details or a paragraph that would work better in another part of your essay, make adjustments.

From sentence to sentence and paragraph to paragraph, use transitions that make your essay flow. Words such as those in the following box help guide the reader from one idea to the next. As with details, balance your use of transition words—more than a few can make a personal essay sound like an instruction manual.

As you move from one point to another, be sure to develop your ideas logically. Review chapter 8, for an example of the effective use of transitions. Note that the author doesn't rely on traditional transition words. It is the repetition of the subjects of soccer and the author's grandmother, along with the chronological sequence, which relate the paragraphs to one another.

Once you've written your introduction, check to be sure there is an obvious connection between it and the body of your essay. Don't waste a dynamic start by dumping the reader into a new context that leaves him or her asking, "*Where am I?*" Show clearly why you began as you did.

For example, if you open with a statistic (such as the Valencia oranges

TRANSITION WORDS AND PHRASES		
after	finally	on the contrary
afterwards	first, second, third	on the other hand
after this	for this reason	similarly
another	however	simultaneously
as a result	in addition	subsequently
because	it follows that	then
conversely	moreover	therefore
consequently	nevertheless	though
despite	next	yet

example on page 50), the next sentence should connect the numbers with your own experience. It might be: *My youth group had a hard enough time packing a dozen boxes of oranges a day. It's hard to imagine how much work is required to pack 86 million boxes.*

Strong Finishes: How to Conclude

End your application essay memorably. As with your introduction, you want your conclusion to both stand out and work as an integral part of your essay. Here are three important conclusion pitfalls to avoid:

- **Answering the big questions.** If you wrote about a topic such as world peace or a personal tragedy, resist the temptation to give reasons or solutions. You don't need to explain the nature of evil in the world, or how hunger can be stopped.
- **Using clichés.** Many essays end with *therefore, in conclusion,* or *in summary.* Save transition words to help you make connections in the body of your essay, and end your essay in your own voice, using fresh words and phrases.
- **Summarizing your essay.** This is the biggest blunder—your essay is short enough that you can expect your reader to remember what you wrote a few paragraphs ago. Summaries are boring, and waste an opportunity to leave your reader with something memorable. Instead, you want your conclusion to echo the dynamic start of your essay. How can you achieve that? Consider the following strategies.

In this online exercise, the emphasis is on focus and organization. Your essay should address the prompt and be logically organized, with ideas flowing easily from one to another.

To complete this online activity, go to the **Additional Online Practice** page on page 131 and follow the instructions.

Once you have logged in, click **Start** under the prompt titled:

Expository Essay: Responsibility

Here's the prompt:

Everybody has responsibilities. Social responsibilities are duties people must perform for others. Other responsibilities are personal. These are commitments people keep for themselves. Think about your social and personal responsibilities. Now write to describe what you think is your most important responsibility.

Click in the empty white box under the instructions and begin to type your sample essay response to this prompt. Periodically click **Save** to make sure that your work is not erased!

When you are finished writing your essay, click **Next Page**. If you'd like to review your work before having it scored, click **Back**. If you are happy with your essay and feel it is complete, click **Score My Test**. You will receive an automatic essay score from 1–6. Click on the link titled **View Scoring Guide** to get a better sense of the criteria used to evaluate your essay.

In addition to getting a sense of the mechanical aspects of your essay, take another look at what you have written by clicking on **View Essay**.

As you check your score, note especially the organization and support results. Your numbers were based on focus, logical order, seamless flow of ideas, development, and relevance. Reread your essay with those characteristics in mind. If you scored less than 6 on either organization or support, review your essay and check for the following:

- Do you have a clear thesis (your most important responsibility)?
- Do your major points describe your responsibility?
- Are those points supported by examples (think *show* rather than *tell*)?
- Is the organization logical, or should parts of the essay be moved, developed more fully, or removed?
- Did you use transitions to move from one idea to another?

Consider rewriting your essay to improve on any weaknesses, taking note of the importance of focus and organization.

- **Continue your essay's discussion.** Propose where it might lead, what it might mean to future generations, and how it might be resolved.
- **Make sense of what happened.** If you told a story that would benefit from an explanation of what it means to you in larger terms, take a few sentences to explain. What did you learn? How will you benefit from the experience?
- **Connect your content with the desire for a college education.** What does your essay say about your decision to apply to a specific college?
- **Echo—but don't repeat—your introduction.** This helps to provide balance. Use some of the same words, phrases, or ideas mentioned in your first paragraph.
- **Bring the reader to the present day.** This works especially well if you wrote about something that happened in your past. What does it say about who you are now? How has it influenced the plans you are making for the future?
- **If it works, end with a famous quote.** Be certain the quote substantiates what you've written, and speaks obviously and poignantly on your topic.
- **Link your discussion to a wider context.** For example, your week-long hands-on experience with a small group of migrant farm workers could conclude with a paragraph on the nature of the issues they face.

Endings that Work

The author of the essay found on page 108 concludes by making sense of what happened. She explains what she takes away from the events described in the essay.

> *Friday afternoon. I am on my way home, staring out the car window, seeing yet not seeing the trees rush by. As I reflect back on the past few days, I realize that I have grown. There is a strength within me that held firm through a pair of difficult events that came to me simultaneously. I can call on that strength when I need it in the future, as I continue to strive for success.*

In the conclusion to her essay, the writer continues her discussion. She expands the lesson about familiar landscapes to encompass those that are unfamiliar or as yet unmade.

> *Wessels has not only permitted me to read the forested landscape at home, to constantly observe and note details of familiar woods to give me a story,*

but he has also allowed me to question the lands I've never been to before, and let me imagine and speculate vast forests of the future, places that have never been, and may never be, save for the realm of imagination.

Watch What You Read

What you read can influence what you write. Syntax and style can improve when you add some great writing to your reading diet. This trick is too simple not to follow. Once you get in the habit, keep it up!

From the beginning of your essay writing process, you should be aware of what you're reading. The phrase *garbage in, garbage out* applies: if you are reading a steady diet of mediocre writing, you are missing a great opportunity to improve your own writing.

The point is not that you will copy the good writing you read, but that it will be a positive influence. Your style, structure, and even vocabulary can improve when you are exposed to high quality writing. Therefore, if your literary diet consists of enticing yet averagely written novels or flashy entertainment magazines, put them aside for a while and pick up something new.

What should you read? We've polled English professors and teachers, college counselors, and admissions officers for their ideas. In the following list are books and periodicals that offer pieces on current events, celebrities, book reviews, science, history, sports, and other topics. Choose material that appeals to you; there is no need to force yourself to read about something that holds little personal interest. You can be assured of finding superior writing on a wide variety of subjects in the following:

- *Rolling Stone* (weekly magazine): essays, fiction, and reporting on political, literary, cultural, and scientific affairs.
- *Vanity Fair* (monthly magazine): reporting and commentary on contemporary issues, fiction, and columns on politics, celebrities, and more.
- *The Economist* (daily newspaper): London publication covering world news, finance and economics, science and technology, books and arts, and business news.
- *The New Yorker* (weekly magazine): political and business reporting, social commentary, fiction, humor, art, poetry, and criticism.
- *Best American Essays 2009*, Mary Oliver, editor (Mariner Books, 2009): annual publication; any year is fine; all volumes include a wide range of subjects.

- *One Hundred Great Essays, 4th edition*, Robert Diyanni (Longman, 2010): great variety of classic and contemporary writing, including works by Queen Elizabeth I, Benjamin Franklin, Zora Neale Hurston, Amy Tan, and Dave Barry.
- *The Best American Magazine Writing of 2009*, American Society of Magazine Editors (Columbia University Press, 2009): includes fiction and reporting on science, sports, current events, and personalities.

ESSAY WRITING WORKSHOP— PART ONE

"The most valuable of all talents is that of never using two words when one will do."

—THOMAS JEFFERSON

You don't have to have perfect command of SAT vocabulary to write a great essay. But you do need to choose your words wisely. Used well, they convey meaning, tone, and style. But misused, words can confuse, annoy, or put your reader to sleep. In this chapter, we'll examine the syntax issues you need to understand to write a great essay.

Get Concise

One of the most common problems with high school writing rarely registers with students. After years of completing assignments with specific word count requirements, students are often in the habit of extending their arguments with dozens of unnecessary words and phrases to make the count. Since the typical college application essay is between 250 and 500 words, and because it is imperative that you tell a compelling story about yourself, now is the time to pare down your writing. Leave out common clutter words and phrases, and get to the point to make your essay strong.

SAT TIP

Wordiness is a favorite error in multiple-choice questions in the Writing section of the SAT. Get in the habit of being concise, and you'll be able to correctly answer more questions and score more points.

Four Phrases to Avoid

The following four worst phrase offenders are all too well known and used. They should be eliminated from your writing because they either aren't necessary, or are awkward and should be altered to a shorter form.

1. *Because of the fact that.*
   In most cases, *because* alone will do.
   - **Instead of:** Because of the fact that it rained, the game was canceled.
   - **Write:** Because it rained, the game was canceled.

2. *That* and *which* phrases.
   Eliminate them by turning the idea in the *that* or *which* phrase into an adjective.
   - **Instead of:** This was a course that was very helpful.
   - **Write:** This was a very helpful course.
   - **Instead of:** The game, which lasted three hours, ended at nine.
   - **Write:** The three-hour game ended at nine.

3. *There is, it is.*
   These constructions avoid the direct approach and are often unnecessary. Drop them and replace with a clear agent of action.
   - **Instead of:** It was with regret that I left the school for the last time.
   - **Write:** I left the school for the last time with regret.
   - **Instead of:** There is no reason I can find to make another choice.
   - **Write:** I can find no reason to make another choice.

4. *That* by itself is a word that often clutters sentences unnecessarily, as in the following example: *He said that he thought that my contribution was useful and that he was happy that there will be more opportunities for me to get involved.*

Word Choices for Concise Writing

Use the following list to revise or delete wordy phrases and improve the effectiveness of your writing.

Wordy	Replace With
a lot of	many or much
all of a sudden	suddenly
along the lines of	like
are able to	can
as a matter of fact	in fact
as a person	(delete)
as a whole	(delete)
as the case may be	(delete)
at the present time	currently or now
basic necessity	necessity
both of these	both
by and large	(delete)
by definition	(delete)
compare and contrast	compare
due to the fact that	because
final destination	destination
for all intents and purposes	(delete)
has a tendency to	often
has the ability to	can
in order to	to
in the event that	if
in the near future	soon
is able to	can
it is clear that	(delete)

Wordy	Replace With
last but not least	finally
on a daily basis	daily
on account of the fact that	because
particular	(delete)
period of time	time
somewhere in the neighborhood of	about
take action	act
the fact that	that
the majority of	most
the reason why	the reason
through the use of	through
totally obvious	obvious
with regard to	regarding
with the exception of	except for

Another way to make certain your writing is concise is to check for the repetition of ideas and information. Saying the same thing more than once can really bore your reader. Writers often repeat themselves unnecessarily because they are not sure they've been clear, or they're not attentive to the need to be concise. Get it right the first time, be confident, and move on.

Repetition in your application essay can take two forms: *word choice* and *content*. Word choice refers to the use of unnecessary words and phrases that simply repeat information already given. For example:

- **Repetitive:** The awards ceremony was held at 4 p.m. in the afternoon.
- **Concise:** The awards ceremony was held at 4 p.m.
- **Repetitive:** As I pointed out in my list of extracurricular activities, I was elected to student council for four years in a row, and during two of those years I was the president.
- **Concise:** I was elected to student council for four years, and spent two years as president.

Content refers to the personal information you are writing about. The essay is not the place to repeat information that can be found elsewhere on your application. For instance, you have already listed your extracurricular activities and GPA, and they have been noted by the admissions committee. There is no need to remind them of these accomplishments. Use your essay to tell your readers something they don't already know about you.

Correcting Repetitive Sentences

Review the following repetitive sentence corrections and avoid making these mistakes in your essay.

- **Repetitious:** It is essential that everyone arrive promptly and on time.
- **Concise:** It is essential that everyone arrive on time.

- **Repetitious:** It's time to terminate the project and put an end to it.
- **Concise:** It's time to terminate the project.

- **Repetitious:** While I was in the all-state orchestra I played first violin and beat out all the other violinists for first chair.
- **Concise:** I played first violin in the all-state orchestra.

Be Precise

Once you've eliminated clutter words and phrases, you want to be certain that your word choices deliver the maximum impact. Choosing appropriate adjectives and adverbs (modifiers) make your points clear and convey ideas with greater style and more shades of meaning. Consider the difference between these two sentences:

> *"A well chosen word has often sufficed to stop a flying army, to change defeat into victory, and to save an empire."*
>
> —EMILE DE GIRARDIN

- Tom puts his hat on, and walks away.
- Tom Wessels slaps his felt hat over his bushy hair, and starts striding away with the confident gait of a hiker.

The latter example allows you to hear the full voice of the writer, and provides a more interesting picture of the action. The first sentence is simply dull. Using modifiers brings your reader more closely into your story, and helps create an important visual and/or emotional connection that makes your writing more powerful and memorable.

Examples of Powerful, Precise Adjectives and Adverbs

Review the following phrases. They're strong examples of effective essay word choices.

- directly involved
- unflagging dedication
- promptly accepted
- productive discussion
- grueling game
- instinctively aware
- influential teacher
- invaluable learning experience

Be Accurate

Pay attention to the meaning of every word you use in your essay. There are many English words that look and/or sound similar, but have very different meanings. If you are unsure of a definition, look it up. One wrong word—using *illicit* when you mean *elicit*, for example—can completely change the meaning of an otherwise well-written sentence. A number of these errors can also make your reader question your grasp of the language.

> *"The difference between the right word and the almost right word is the difference between lightning and a lightning bug."*
>
> —MARK TWAIN

The following is a list of commonly confused word pairs or groups, with brief definitions. Check your essay for them, making sure you have used the correct word. You might want to make flash cards for each pair or group, and use them so your future writing improves.

Confusing Words	Quick Definition
accept	recognize
except	excluding
access	means of approaching
excess	extra
affect	to influence
effect (noun)	result
effect (verb)	to bring about
assure	to make certain (assure someone)
ensure	to make certain
insure	to make certain (financial value)
beside	next to
besides	in addition to
bibliography	list of writings
biography	a life story
complement	match
compliment	praise
decent	well-mannered
descent	decline, fall
desert	arid, sandy region
dessert	sweet served after a meal
disburse	to pay
disperse	to spread out
disinterested	no strong opinion either way
uninterested	don't care
elicit	to stir up
illicit	illegal

Confusing Words	Quick Definition
farther	beyond (distance)
further	additional (amount)
imply	hint, suggest
infer	assume, deduce
personal	pertaining to the individual
personnel	employees
principal (adjective)	main
principal (noun)	person in charge
principle	standard
than	in contrast to
then	next
their	belonging to them
there	in a place
they're	they are
who	substitute for he, she, or they
whom	substitute for him, her, or them
your	belonging to you
you're	you are

Choosing the right words also means being aware of the many commonly misused ones. You may find examples of misused words in the media, on billboards and other signs, in speech, and in everyday writing. In fact, even when used incorrectly, these words often sound acceptable to many writers. But they will stand out to admissions officers as glaring errors. Take the time to review the following words and avoid embarrassing mistakes.

Word	Meaning
among	a comparison or reference to three or more people or things
between	a comparison or reference to two people or things
amount	when you cannot count the items to which you are referring, and when referring to singular nouns
number	when you can count the items to which you are referring, and when referring to plural nouns
anxious	nervous
eager	enthusiastic, or looking forward to something
bring	moving something toward the speaker
take	moving something away from the speaker [**Hint:** remember, bring *to*, take *away*]
can	used to state ability
may	used to state permission
each other	when referring to two people or things
one another	when referring to three or more people or things (e.g. an abbreviation for the Latin "exempli gratia," meaning *free example* or *for example*)
i.e.	an abbreviation for the Latin "id est," meaning *it is* or *that is*
feel bad	used when talking about emotional feelings
feel badly	used when talking about physically feeling something
fewer	when you can count the items
less	when you cannot count the items
good	an adjective, which describes a person, place, or thing

Word	Meaning
well	an adverb, which describes an action or verb
its	belonging to *it*
it's	contraction of *it is*
lay	the action of placing or putting an item somewhere; a transitive verb, meaning something you do *to* something else
lie	to recline or be placed (a lack of action); an intransitive verb, meaning it does not act on anything or anyone else
more	used to compare one thing to another
most	used to compare one thing to more than one other thing
that	a pronoun that introduces a restrictive (or essential) clause
which	a pronoun that introduces a non-restrictive (or unessential) clause

Stay Active

> *"You have such strong words at command, that they make the smallest argument seem formidable."*
>
> —GEORGE ELIOT

When a verb is active, the subject of the sentence *performs* an action. In a passive construction, the subject *receives* the action. Consider the following:

Active: The bird ate the birdseed.
Passive: The birdseed was eaten by the bird.

In the first sentence, the subject (*the bird*) performs the action (*ate*). In the second sentence, does the subject (*birdseed*) do anything? No; instead it is acted upon.

Note how many more words it takes to communicate the same idea in the passive voice. This is one reason the active voice is preferred, especially in your application essay. It is more direct and concise. Take a look at the following examples:

- **Instead of:** The bank account was closed by Sheila.
- **Write:** Sheila closed the bank account.

- **Instead of:** The active voice should be used by essay writers.
- **Write:** Essay writers should use the active voice.

That said, there are some instances when you should use the passive voice. Choose it when:

- you want to deliberately emphasize the receiver of the action instead of the performer
  Example: My fender was dented three times in that parking lot.
- the performer is unknown
  Example: Mani's wallet was mysteriously returned.
- you want to avoid mentioning the performer of the action
  Example: The experiment resulted in a new theory.

Eliminate Ambiguity

> *"Speak clearly, if you speak at all; carve every word before you let it fall."*
>
> —Oliver Wendell Holmes

Using ambiguous words (that is, words with two or more possible meanings), or using the right words in the wrong order, can cause confusion. The meaning understood by the reader may not be the one intended by the writer. Here are two important guidelines to follow in order to avoid ambiguity:

1. Refrain from using words and phrases with more than one meaning.

2. Be sure the words you use are in the right order to convey your intended meaning.

Let's take a look at a few examples:

> **Confusing:** During my photojournalism class, I shot the model.
> **Revised:** During my photojournalism class, I took pictures of the model.

The first sentence can be read two ways: you shot pictures with a camera, or you shot the model with a gun. This kind of confusion can happen whenever a word has more than one possible meaning. The second choice eliminates the confusion.

> **Confusing:** My customer ate the sandwich with the blue hat.
> **Revised:** My customer with the blue hat ate the sandwich.

Here, the word order of the sentence causes the confusion. Did the customer eat her sandwich with her hat? Because the phrase *with the blue hat* is in the wrong place, the meaning of the sentence is unclear. The second choice eliminates the confusion.

Correcting Ambiguous Language

Review the following ambiguous sentences and clarifications, which will help you to avoid making similar mistakes on your essay.

- **Ambiguous:** When reaching for the phone, the coffee spilled on the table.
- **Clear:** The coffee spilled on the table when you reached for the phone.

- **Ambiguous:** I went to see the doctor with a severe headache.
- **Clear:** I went to see the doctor because I had a severe headache.

- **Ambiguous:** The famous artist drew stares when he entered the room.
- **Clear:** The famous artist received stares when he entered the room.

- **Ambiguous:** When writing on the computer, the spell checker often comes in handy.
- **Clear:** The spell checker often comes in handy when I am writing on the computer.

Don't Offend

Your essay must be free of biased language, including negative stereotypes, which may result in annoying or excluding others. Whether or not its use is intentional (and often it is not), biased language can be offensive. Your goal is to make a positive connection with your reader, rather than to exclude them. Understanding the purpose of inclusive language, and using it in your essay, will assure that your message gets across as

> *"A blow with a word strikes deeper than a blow with a sword."*
>
> —Robert Burton

intended, without causing offense. Replace any possibly offensive words and phrases with inclusive language that doesn't offend or degrade another person.

Gender Bias

Consider the following to avoid gender bias in your essay:

- Avoid the suffix *–ess*, which has the effect of minimizing the significance of the word to which it is attached (*actor* is preferable to *actress*, *proprietor* to *proprietress*).
- Do not overuse *he* and *him*. Instead, use *his* or *her* or *their* and *those*, or alternate between *him* and *her*.
- Degender titles. *Businessman* becomes *businessperson* or *executive*, *chairman* becomes *chair* or *chairperson*, *stewardess* becomes *flight attendant*, *weatherman* becomes *meteorologist*.
- When referring to a couple, don't make any assumptions. *Inappropriate*: Mr. Rosenberg and Caryn, Mr. and Mrs. Bill Rosenberg. *Appropriate*: Mr. Rosenberg and Ms. Fetzer.
- Use professional, rather than personal, descriptive terms. *Inappropriate*: Robin Benoit, a lovely novelist. *Appropriate*: Robin Benoit, an experienced novelist.

Race Bias

Consider the following to avoid race bias in your essay:

- Leave out any reference to race, unless it is relevant to the subject of your writing.
- Focus on a person's individual and professional characteristics and qualifications, not racial characteristics.

Disability Bias

Consider the following to avoid disability bias in your essay:

- Discuss the person, not his or her handicap.
- If your writing is specifically focused on disabilities or disease, or you must mention them for some reason, don't use words that imply victimization or create negative stereotypes.
- Don't use the word *courageous* to describe a person with a disability, unless the context allows the adjective to be used for all. Someone is not courageous because they are deaf, but they may be because they swam the English Channel.
- Always put the person ahead of the disability, as in *person with impaired hearing*, rather than *hearing-impaired person*.

Opening Your Thesaurus—Think Twice

Big words won't win points with your readers. In fact, many admissions officers see them as evidence that you may have been coached, or that your essay isn't your own work. Aim to sound like yourself, not to impress with your knowledge of ten-letter words. There is an important difference between using just the right word to convey meaning, and using a bigger, longer word when a simpler one will do.

> *"For one word a man is often deemed to be wise, and for one word he is often deemed to be foolish. We should indeed be careful what we say."*
>
> —CONFUCIUS

Not convinced yet? Here are a few other reasons to stop looking for and using so-called big words:

- **They sound pretentious.** Remember, you are supposed to sound like you, not a politician or chairman-of-the-board.
- **They can sound ridiculous.** By using words that are not in your normal vocabulary, you run the risk of using them incorrectly.
- **They may seem like a tactic.** Your reader might think you are trying to add weight with words because you are worried your essay isn't well written, or that your ideas aren't worth reading.

Too Much of a Good Thing

Review the following examples of overwrought writing, and avoid making the same mistakes in your essay.

- **Too much:** I was determined to eschew obfuscation by packing only those things that I could transport in one valise.
- **To the point:** I decided to keep it simple by packing only those things that I could carry in one suitcase.

- **Too much:** In secondary school I took my first accounting class and commenced to aid my mother with the accounting functions of the business.
- **To the point:** In high school I took my first accounting class, and began to help my mother with the accounting tasks of the business.

- **Too much:** At my summer employment, I had the fortuity to obtain IT-related information as it pertains to the engineering field.
- **To the point:** At my summer job, I had the chance to learn about Information Technology as it relates to engineering.

> ## INSIDER INFORMATION
>
> *"Some essays put up what I call the red flag. I might be reading something that sounds like an essay I've read before. Or, the essay might not be in the student's voice—something just doesn't sound right. If I see a student whose grades and courses don't seem to match the quality of the writing, that red flag will go up."*
>
> —AUGUSTINE GARZA,
> Deputy Director of Admissions,
> University of Texas—Austin

ESSAY WRITING WORKSHOP— PART TWO

Understanding the word usage issues that can plague high school writers is the first step towards improving your essay. When you know which words to use, and why, you'll be able to tell your story more forcefully, and with greater clarity and precision. There are rules that govern the use of those words, so making sure that you're following them is important. Here, we'll look at the most common errors made by high school writers, and explain how to avoid them.

Grammar Check: A Warning

If you're thinking about skipping this chapter and just running a grammar check on your computer instead, here are a few words of caution: the program isn't foolproof. Grammar programs make mistakes, both by missing errors and by flagging things that are actually correct. They also suggest corrections that are themselves errors. Think your grammar check is better than most? A number of studies comparing the effectiveness of various programs found them to perform about the same (fair to poor).

The first problem, missing errors, is addressed in this chapter. You'll find explanations for the most common types of grammatical mistakes missed by grammar check programs, including comma and apostrophe use, verb tense shifts, vague pronoun references, incorrect pronoun agreement, run-on sentences, and fragments.

When grammar check does highlight an error, it may be a mistake. But if your knowledge of grammar is limited, you won't know whether to accept the correction. To further complicate matters, you may be offered more than one possible correction, and will be asked to choose between them. Unless you're familiar enough with the specific problem, this may be no more than a guess on your part.

While there have been improvements in computer grammar checking, nothing is more effective than a careful review of your writing after using the program. Our list of proofreading tips on page 84 offers a number of great suggestions.

Subject/Verb Agreement

Agreement refers to number—if you have a singular subject, you need a singular verb. Plural subjects take plural verbs. To achieve subject/verb agreement, first determine whether your subject is singular or plural, and then pair it with the correct verb form.

The following examples use the verb *to be*, which is irregular (I am, you are, he/she/it is, they are, I was, you were, he/she/it was, they were):

- **Instead of:** Tim and Fran *is* a great couple.
- **Write:** Tim and Fran *are* a great couple. (*Tim and Fran* is a plural subject that takes a plural verb.)

- **Instead of:** One of my friends *are* going to your school.
- **Write:** One of my friends *is* going to school.(*One* is a singular subject takes a singular verb.)

When it Gets Tricky

Agreement can be difficult to determine when sentences are complex, or when the subject is compound (made up of more than one noun). Common examples include sentences in which the subject follows the verb, and those beginning with *there is* and *there are*, and *here is* and *here are*. When editing your work, remember to first figure out whether your subject is singular or plural, and then match it to the correct verb.

- **Instead of:** There *is* too many meetings scheduled on Tuesday morning.
- **Write:** There *are* too many meetings scheduled on Tuesday morning.

- **Instead of:** Here *are* the report you asked me to write.
- **Write:** Here *is* the report you asked me to write.

When compound subjects are connected by *and* (pencils *and* pens) they are plural. When they're connected by *or* (World War I *or* World War II) they are singular. Confusion can set in when the nouns forming the compound subject are both singular and plural, and are connected by *or*. Here are two examples:

- Lee or his friends are driving too fast.
- Was it his friends or Lee who was driving too fast?

Both sentences are correct, because when you have a compound subject made up of at least one singular subject and one plural subject connected by *or*, the verb must agree with the subject that is closest to it. In the first case, *friends* is plural, so the plural verb *are* is correct. In the second, *Lee* is singular, so the singular *was* is correct.

Run-on Sentences and Fragments

College counselor Susan Goodkin names run-on sentences as one of the most common errors on the admissions essays that she reviews. Run-on sentences are formed by incorrectly joining two or more independent clauses, which are complete sentences that could stand on their own. Take a look at the following sentence:

- I was on the soccer team, however I enjoy playing golf.

This sentence contains two independent clauses: *I was on the soccer team* and *I enjoy playing golf*. Because they can stand alone, they can't be joined with a comma. Run-on sentences can be corrected by breaking them into two or more complete sentences, by adding a conjunction (a connecting word such as *and*, *but*, *yet*, or *so*), or by changing the punctuation.

Here's a corrected version:

- I was on the soccer team, and I also enjoy playing golf.

Let's look at another example:

- When spring break is over, we will get back to work, there will be plenty of studying to do before finals.

The clause *when spring break is over* is correctly attached to *we will get back to work* with a comma. But the second independent clause, *there will be plenty of studying to do before finals* cannot be joined to the first with only a comma. It is a complete sentence that can stand alone, so if it remains part of the longer sentence, it must be connected with a period or semicolon.

Fragments are groups of words that are presented as sentences but lack a subject, a verb, or both. Consider the following:

- The well-dressed man.
- Walked to school in the rain.

In the first fragment, the verb is missing. All we have is a subject. What did the well-dressed man do? In the second fragment, the subject is missing. Who walked in the rain? To correct sentence fragments, determine what is missing (subject or verb) and add it. Note that number of words has nothing to do with distinguishing fragments from sentences—fragments can be long! Let's look at the following:

- **Instead of:** My older sister Ellen, who traveled to Japan.
- **Write:** My older sister Ellen traveled to Japan.

- **Instead of:** Taking a taxi when it is raining to keep her shoes from being ruined by the water.
- **Write:** Taking a taxi when it is raining keeps her shoes from being ruined by the water.

Apostrophe Misuse

Apostrophes are used to form contractions, indicate possession or ownership, and form certain plurals. Eight rules cover all of the situations in which they may appear:

1. **Add *'s* to form the singular possessive, even when the noun ends in *s*:**
   - The *school's* lunchroom needs to be cleaned.
   - The *drummer's* solo received a standing ovation.
   - *Mr. Perkins's* persuasive essay was very convincing.

2. **A few plurals, not ending in *s*, also form the possessive by adding *'s*:**
   - The *children's* toys were found in every room of the house.
   - The line for the *women's* restroom was too long.
   - *Men's* shirts come in a variety of neck sizes.

3. **Possessive plural nouns already ending in *s* need only the apostrophe added:**
   - The *customers'* access codes are confidential.
   - The *students'* grades improved each semester.
   - The flight *attendants'* uniforms were blue and white.

4. **Indefinite pronouns show ownership by the addition of *'s*:**
   - *Everyone's* hearts were in the right place.
   - *Somebody's* dog was barking all night.
   - It was *no one's* fault that we lost the game.

5. **Possessive pronouns never have apostrophes, even though some may end in *s*:**
   - *Our* car is up for sale.
   - *Your* garden is beautiful.
   - *His* handwriting is difficult to read.

6. **Use an *'s* to form the plurals of letters, figures, and numbers used as words, as well as certain expressions of time and money:**
   - She has a hard time pronouncing *s's*.
   - My street address contains three *5's*.
   - The project was the result of a *year's* worth of work.

7. **Show possession in the last word when using names of organizations and businesses, in hyphenated words, and in joint ownership:**

USING IT

The number one apostrophe error occurs with the simple word *it*. The addition of *'s* to the word *it* doesn't form the possessive, but rather the contraction *it's*, meaning *it is*. The possessive form of the word (meaning *belonging to it*) has no apostrophe. If you're not sure which one to use, substitute *it is*—if it works, you need the apostrophe.

- *Sam and Janet's* graduation was three months ago.
- I went to visit my *great-grandfather's* alma mater.
- *The Future Farmers of America's* meeting was moved to Monday.

8. **Apostrophes form contractions by taking the place of the missing letter or number.**
   - *We're* going out of town next week.
   - *She's* going to write the next proposal.
   - My supervisor was in the class of *'89.*

Comma Misuse

Misplacing commas, or leaving them out when they're called for, can confuse meaning and create sloppy writing. The following six rules will guide you in the correct usage of commas.

1. **Use a comma to separate items in a series, including the last two items.**
   This comma is known as the serial comma.
   - **Right:** To my parents, Ayn Rand, and God.
   - **Wrong:** To my parents, Ayn Rand and God.

2. **Use a comma with the conjunctions *for, and, nor, but, or,* and *yet*.** *Remember the mnemonic FANBOY to join two independent clauses.*
   - He left for the Bahamas, but she went to Mexico.
   - I am neither excited about the idea, nor am I even thinking about using it.

3. **Use a comma to separate adjectives when the word *and* makes sense between them.**
   - That was the most depressing, poorly directed movie I've ever seen!
   - Wrong: It was a bleak, November day.
   - Wrong: He wore a bright, red tie.

4. **Use a comma after introductory phrases.**
   - Since she is leaving on vacation next Friday, she scheduled a replacement for her shift.
   - As the group considered the effect of the gas tax, they asked many citizens to share their opinions.

5. **Use commas to set off words and phrases that are not an integral part of the sentence.**
    - Jill, Jack's wife, works at the bank.
    - Henry's penchant for one-liners, while annoying to his family, delights his friends.

6. **Use commas to set off quotations, dates, and titles.**
    - Napoleon is said to have remarked, "The word 'impossible' is not in my dictionary."
    - On July 4, 1776, the United States of America declared its independence.
    - Robert Zia, MD, is my general practitioner.

BE CAREFUL

Commas can create grammatical errors. When two complete sentences are joined by a comma, thus creating a run-on sentence, the error is called a comma splice. To correct it:

- replace the comma with a period, forming two sentences.
- replace the comma with a semicolon.
- join the two clauses with a conjunction such as *and*, *because*, or *so*.

Accidental Shifts

Shifts are movements from one form to another. In grammar, the three most common shifts involve verb tenses, pronouns, and the active/passive voice. When these movements are made accidentally, they can cause confusion. Shifts are also one of the College Board's favorite grammatical errors—expect to see a few examples in the SAT Writing section.

Verb tenses must be consistent within each sentence and paragraph. Because they represent time (past, present, and future), shifting them can cause confusion. Consider the following:

- If you make a mistake, your grade went down.

If you make a mistake refers to something that may happen in the future. But *grade went down* is in the past tense. We don't know if the speaker is referring to something that already happened, or something that may happen. The key to avoiding verb tense shifts is to be aware of the tense you're writing in, and use it consistently. Consider the following:

- **Instead of:** I had never been to London, but I will feel right at home there.
- **Write:** I had never been to London, but I felt right at home there.

- **Instead of:** Last year, the governor said he is campaigning for our candidate.
- **Write:** Last year, the governor said he would campaign for our candidate.

Pronouns take the place of nouns and may be masculine or feminine, singular or plural. Shifting pronoun types within a sentence is another way to confuse your reader. Consider the following:

- If they want to succeed, one should study diligently for tests.

The pronoun *they* is plural, but *one* is singular. The reader has to guess: is the author speaking about a group or an individual? Correcting shifts in pronouns means being aware of whether the subject you're replacing is singular or plural, masculine or feminine. The pronoun *one* is often at the root of the problem. It's often easiest to keep pronouns from shifting by replacing one or more of them with a more specific word. Here are a couple of examples:

- **Instead of:** If one is careful, they can avoid additional cable television fees.
- **Write:** If cable television subscribers are careful, they can avoid additional fees.

- **Instead of:** We asked about interest rates for our mortgage, and found out you could lock in at any time.
- **Write:** We asked about interest rates for our mortgage, and found out we could lock in at any time.

The third type of shift occurs when moving incorrectly from the active to passive voice, or vice versa. In the active voice, the subject of the sentence performs the action; in the passive voice, the subject receives the action. Keep in mind that in most situations, the active voice is preferred. To correct the shift, change the passive part of the sentence to match the active one. Consider the following:

- Lea bought the sushi, and it was eaten by her children.

In this example, the first part of the sentence is written in the active voice; the subject (*Lea*) performs the action (*bought*). However, in the second part, the subject (*it*, or *the sushi*) receives the action (*was eaten*). To continue the active voice, the sentence should be corrected to read:

- Lea bought the sushi, and her children ate it.

Dangling and Misplaced Modifiers

Dangling and misplaced modifiers, though sometimes difficult to recognize, are easily fixed by rearranging word order. A dangling modifier is a phrase or clause, using a verb ending in *–ing,* that does not refer to the subject of the sentence it modifies. Take a look at the following:

- **Instead of:** While working on his English assignment, Tony's computer crashed. (Was the computer working on the assignment?)
- **Write:** While Tony was working on his English assignment, his computer crashed.

Note that correcting a dangling modifier involves adding and/or rearranging the words in a sentence to make the meaning clear. Let's look at another example:

- **Instead of:** Having been recently fixed, Pedro was able to use the bicycle pump this morning. (Was Pedro recently fixed?)
- **Write:** Since the bicycle pump was recently fixed, Pedro was able to use it this morning.

A misplaced modifier is a word or phrase that describes something, but is in the wrong place in the sentence. It isn't dangling and no extra words are needed, the modifier is just in the wrong place. The danger of misplaced modifiers, as with dangling modifiers, is that they confuse meaning. Here's an example:

- I had to have the cafeteria unlocked meeting with student government this morning.

Did the cafeteria meet with student government? To say exactly what is meant, the modifying phrase *meeting with student government* should be moved to the beginning of the sentence, as follows:

- Meeting with student government this morning, I had to have the cafeteria unlocked.

Unclear Pronoun References

Recall that pronouns, such as *me, you, he,* and *she,* replace nouns. But when it's not clear what noun the pronoun has replaced or refers to, the meaning of the sentence can get confused. For example:

■ I went to school every day with Ted and Fred, and we took his car.

Whose car? *His* could mean either Ted's or Fred's. The writer needs to use a proper name instead of a pronoun in order to eliminate the possibility that the reader will not understand him or her. Correct it this way:

■ I went to school every day with Ted and Fred, and we took Ted's car.

Here's another example:

■ They considered publishing our poems in the anthology.

Using a vague *they* when there are specific people behind an action is another common pronoun error. In this case, the writer doesn't know exactly who those people are. However, even without that information, the sentence can be revised to be more precise:

■ The publishing company considered publishing our poems in their anthology.

Here are a few more examples:

■ **Instead of:** They passed new environmental legislation yesterday.
■ **Write:** The senate passed new environmental legislation yesterday.

■ **Instead of:** Mr. Jones told James that he had found his missing report.
■ **Write:** Mr. Jones told James that he had found James' missing report.

■ **Instead of:** They closed the movie theater after they discovered several fire code violations.
■ **Write:** The owners of the movie theater closed their doors after they discovered several fire code violations.

Spelling

Some people seem to have inherited good spelling genes. However, if you don't fall into that category, there are a number of basic rules and techniques you can learn to improve your ability to spell.

Tempted to rely on your computer's spell check? While there's no excuse not to use it—it's fast, simple, and catches many common spelling errors—it's not pefect. Be aware of its most important limitations:

- **Nonword versus real word errors.** Most of us think of spelling errors in the first category—a string of letters that doesn't make a real word. You might type *sevn* instead of *seven*, or *th* for *the*. Spell check is an excellent tool for catching these types of mistakes. However, what if you're writing about the seven other students who participated in the Thirty Hour march, and you leave off the *s and* type *even*? This is known as a real word error. You have typed a legitimate, correctly spelled word; it's just not the word you meant to type and it doesn't convey the meaning you intended. Spell check can't find these types of errors.

- **Proper nouns.** Spell check uses a dictionary that doesn't include most proper nouns and words in other categories, such as the names of chemicals. You can always add a word or words to the dictionary once you're sure of its spelling, but for the first time, you will need to use another source (a reliable print one is best) to verify the spelling.

- **Errors spelled similarly to another real word.** If you misspell a word in such a way that it is now closer to a word other than the one you intended, spell check will probably offer the wrong word as a possible correction. For example, if your essay includes a coffee house scenario, and you type the word *expresso*, spell check will correct the error with *express* rather than *espresso*. Similarly, *alot* will be changed to *allot*. You must pay careful attention to spell check's suggested corrections to ensure the right selection.

Basic Spelling Rules

Carefully review the following basic spelling rules, and be sure to avoid making these mistakes in your essay.

1. **I Before E.** *This rule is familiar to most spellers, but they don't always follow it:* "*I before* E *except after* C, *or when sounding like* A *as in* neighbor *or* weigh." *That's why* convenient, grievance, *and* lenient, *are always on lists of commonly misspelled words.*
   - **After C:** *ceiling, conceit, conceive, deceit, deceive, perceive, receipt, receive*
   - **When sounding like A:** *beige, eight, freight, neighbor, sleigh, vein, weigh, feint*
   - **Exceptions:** The rule has exceptions, which you should learn— *conscience, counterfeit, either, foreign, forfeit, height, leisure, neither, science, seize, seizure, species, sufficient, weird*

2. **Doubling Final Consonants.** *Final consonants are doubled when adding a suffix in two situations:*
   - When the ending begins with a vowel (*-ing, -ed, -age, -er, -ence, -ance,* and *-al*): *hitter, occurrence, stoppage, running*
   - When the last syllable of the word is accented and ends in a single consonant preceded by a single vowel: *beginning, incurred, transmittal*

3. **Dealing With Final E's.** *There are four possibilities when adding a suffix to a word ending with a silent -e:*
   - When adding a suffix that begins with a vowel (*-able, -ing, -ed, -er*) drop the silent *-e: advancing, larger, movable*

     Exception: When a final *e* is preceded by a soft *g* or *c*, or a long *o*, the *e* is kept to maintain proper pronunciation: *courageous* (the *g* would have a hard sound if the *e* was dropped), *hopeful* (the *o* would have a soft sound if the *e* was dropped), *changeable, noticeable*

PROOFREADING TRICKS TO CATCH SPELLING ERRORS

The following techniques can help you catch what spell check can't:

- **Take your time.** Studies show that waiting at least twenty minutes before proofreading your work can increase your likelihood of finding errors. Get up from your computer, take a break, or move on to some other task, and then come back to your writing.
- **Read backward.** Go through your writing from the last word to the first, focusing on each individual word rather than on the context.
- **Ask for help.** A pair of fresh eyes may find mistakes that you have overlooked dozens of times.
- **Go under cover.** Print out a draft copy of your writing, and read it with a blank piece of paper over it, revealing just one sentence at a time. This technique will encourage a careful line-by-line edit.
- **Watch the speed limit.** No matter which proofreading technique(s) you use, take it slow. Reading at your normal speed won't give you enough time to spot errors.
- **Know thyself.** Keep track of the kinds of mistakes you typically make. Common spelling errors can be caught by spell check if you add the word or words to the spell check dictionary. When you know what you are looking for, you are more likely to find it.

- When adding a suffix that begins with a consonant (*-ful*, *-less*, *-ly*, *-ment*, *-ness*), keep the final *e*: *amusement, suspenseful, likeness*
- If a final silent *e* is preceded by another vowel, drop the *e* when adding any ending: *argue* becomes *argument* or *argued*, *true* becomes *truly*

4. **Forming Plurals.** *Plurals are formed in five ways:*
   - Add an *s* to most words: *chairs, monkeys, rodeos*
   - Add an *es* to words ending in *x, s, sh,* or *ch*: *churches, foxes, dishes*
   - When a word ends in a consonant plus *y*, change *y* to *ie* and add *s*: *babies, enemies, discrepancies*
   - Add *es* to nouns ending in a long *o* preceded by a consonant (other than musical terms): *buffaloes, embargoes, tomatoes, heroes, mosquitoes, dominoes, volcanoes, potatoes* (compare to *pianos, sopranos, solos*)
   - For many words ending in *f* or *fe*, change *f* or *fe* to *v* and add *s* or *es*: *calves, elves, knives, leaves, lives, loaves, thieves, wives, wolves*

5. **Using -cede, -ceed, and –sede.** *Only one English word ends in* –sede: supersede. *Only three end in* –ceed: exceed, proceed, *and* succeed. *All others use* -cede.

The 150 Most Commonly Misspelled Words

Use this list as the basis for starting your own word list. Circle each word that you usually misspell, and add other words that you find especially troublesome. Keep it available for quick reference when you're writing.

absence	basically	conscientious
abundance	boundary	consistent
accidentally	bulletin	convenient
accommodate	calendar	correspondence
acknowledgment	canceled	deceive
acquaintance	cannot	definitely
aggravate	cemetery	dependent
alibi	coincidence	depot
alleged	collectible	descend
ambiguous	committee	desperate
analysis	comparative	development
annual	completely	dilemma
argument	condemn	discrepancy
awkward	congratulations	eighth

eligible	lightning	receipt
embarrass	loophole	receive
equivalent	losing	recommend
euphoria	maintenance	reference
existence	maneuver	referred
exuberance	mathematics	regardless
feasible	millennium	relevant
February	minuscule	religious
fifth	miscellaneous	remembrance
forcibly	misspell	reservoir
forfeit	negotiable	responsible
formerly	ninth	restaurant
fourth	occasionally	rhythm
fulfill	occurred	ridiculous
grateful	omission	roommate
grievance	opportunity	scary
guarantee	outrageous	scissors
guidance	pamphlet	secretary
harass	parallel	separate
hindrance	perceive	souvenir
ideally	permanent	specifically
implement	perseverance	sufficient
independence	personnel	supersede
indispensable	possess	temperament
inoculate	potato	temperature
insufficient	precede	truly
interference	preferred	twelfth
interrupt	prejudice	ubiquitous
jealousy	prevalent	unanimous
jewelry	privilege	usually
judgment	procedure	usurp
leisure	proceed	vacuum
length	prominent	vengeance
lenient	pronunciation	visible
liaison	quandary	Wednesday
lieutenant	questionnaire	wherever

Memorization Techniques

The best ways to remember how to spell vocabulary words is to practice using them and memorize them. Here are three approaches:

1. **Create mnemonics.** Creating mnemonics is a great way to improve your spelling. You might remember how to spell *separate* by recalling that it contains a *rat*. *Cemetery* has three *e*'s in it, as in *eeek*. The final vowel in stationery is an *e*, as in *envelope*.

2. **Organize and reorganize your list of misspelled words.** Group words with the same beginnings or endings, with double vowels, or with double consonants. Use these grouping strategies or come up with your own ways to organize your words.

3. **Take a traditional spelling test.** Give your list to a friend. As he or she reads the words aloud, write them down. Create a shorter list of only those words you misspelled on the test, and work on memorizing those.

FINALIZING AND SUBMITTING THE ESSAY

Once you have a rough draft of your essay, you're ready to transform it into a polished piece of writing. The polishing process consists of three steps: revising, editing, and proofreading. Bring out the magnifying lens you used to narrow and focus your content; it's needed again.

Revision lets you look at your essay as a whole; pay attention to the main issues involved in its crafting. Have you addressed the topic? Is there a logical flow to your ideas or story? Is each paragraph necessary and properly placed?

Editing brings the magnifying lens closer, allowing you to look closely at words and sentences. Are your word choices appropriate and fresh? Are there any repetitive or awkward sentences or phrases?

Finally, the proofreading step magnifies even closer. You will check each word for errors in spelling, and also correct any other mechanics mistakes, such as grammar and punctuation.

In the final chapter, you'll see actual student essays with feedback describing what worked, what didn't, and how revisions and edits could improve them. By studying these essays and the comments that follow them, you'll get a much better idea of how to finalize your own essay.

Many writers are tempted to skip the revising, editing, and proofreading steps. They may feel intimidated by the thought of reworking their writing, and hope that their essays are good enough. But this process doesn't have to be difficult. This chapter includes many ideas that you can use to quickly improve the quality of your writing. The bottom line: there is no excuse for submitting a personal statement that is not the very best writing you are capable of.

Revising

Revision, meaning to visit or look at again, is the most general reexamination of your essay. The process can seem overwhelming—you need to look at your entire essay with fresh eyes and ears, check to see if you have achieved your goal, and decide if any sections of the essay need improving. There's no need to worry; breaking it down into four parts (one of which simply involves waiting) makes it more manageable:

1. **Put down your essay and don't look at it for at least one day before revising.**

2. **Read it through once and imagine you're reading it for the first time.**

3. **Note your reactions to the essay and answer the following:**
   - Does the content of your essay address or match the topic?
   - What does your essay say about you? Does it tell the admissions committee something they couldn't have learned from the rest of your application?
   - Will your essay help you stand out against those who have similar GPAs, class ranks, and test scores? Is it memorable and interesting?
   - Would any reader(s) understand everything you've written, or are some points in need of clarification?
   - Is your introduction a good hook that draws the reader into the essay, or should it be eliminated or rewritten?

- Does your writing flow? Does it follow a logical progression with each paragraph and point made in the right place?
- Is your writing personal? Does it sound like you, or could it have been written by someone else?
- Does your conclusion make sense? Does it make a lasting impact or is it just a wrap-up of what you've already said?

4. **Make any necessary changes, and be willing to add and/or remove writing that isn't working.**
   - Word processing makes revising easy; make changes, see if they improve the essay, and then save the changes or try again.
   - Consider adding colorful anecdotes.
   - Remove any unnecessary adjectives.
   - Replace ambiguous language with more precise words and phrases.
   - Delete anything that is not relevant to and distracts from your point.
   - Move paragraphs, sentences, and words if they fit better somewhere else.

Editing

Editing your essay means checking, and improving when necessary, the words you've chosen and the sentences in which those words appear. As you edit, you'll read through each paragraph a number of times, paying careful attention to

A WORD ABOUT PLAGIARISM

You are probably aware of the many Internet sites offering essays for sale, and resources claiming they have essays that work. What you may not realize is that admissions committees know about them too. In fact, they can easily check suspicious essays against those found on the Internet and published in books. Having even a phrase or two in common with one of these essays constitutes plagiarism.

Plagiarism is a serious academic offense, and will disqualify you from consideration by the school(s) to which you're applying. It's too high a price to pay after all of the work you've done to get yourself this far. The advice is simple: write your own essay, one that provides a glimpse into who you are and what you're about. Your ideas and your words must be your own.

sentences and the words that comprise them. While some students can edit effectively on the computer, others find it easier to use a hard copy of their essay. Unlike revising, which entails the possible reworking of large parts of your essay, editing is a word-by-word and sentence-by-sentence task. Taking pen to paper may help you focus more closely on the pieces that make up your essay, rather than the work as a whole.

As you read your essay, ask yourself the following questions. Circle any problems as you encounter them. You might also want to make a quick note in the margin with ideas about how to fix the problem(s).

- Are all of your ideas and details necessary? Do they relate appropriately to the topic?
- Do you repeat yourself? Rework your point so that you say it well the first time, and remove any repetitious words and phrases.
- Do you have enough details? Look through your essay for generalities, and make them more specific.
- Do you reinforce each point with a concrete and/or personal example?
- Is your sentence structure varied? Sentences should not all be the same length, nor should they all be repetitive in any other way, such as all beginning with *I*.
- Are there any clichés or other types of overused language?
- Do you use the active voice whenever possible?
- Are there too many or too few adjectives and adverbs?

After you've read through your essay a few times and highlighted any areas that need improving, focus on one problem at a time. For example, if a point isn't made clearly and directly, or if it's too general, add a phrase or a sentence to clear it up. Notice how the edit of the following sentence moves it from telling to showing.

- **Telling:** I stay in shape for my sports teams all year.
- **Showing:** I stay physically active during the year. I play football and basketball, and in the off-season run and lift weights.

The first sentence is vague, and tells very little about the author. By adding the specific things the writer does to stay in shape year-round, the reader better understands the point, and the writer.

If you're starting to worry about every idea, word, and comma, take a deep breath and relax. While your goal should be to produce an error-free essay that's written as well as you're able to make it, many admissions counselors say they'd rather read an interesting and unique essay rather than a perfect one that reveals nothing about its writer.

> **INSIDER INFORMATION**
>
> *"We read holistically. In fact, we were trained by the professor who developed the scoring rubric for the SAT essay. A couple of stray errors won't be held against you."*
>
> —AUGUSTINE GARZA,
> University of Texas—Austin

In some instances, your point may get lost if you go off on a tangent, or include information that doesn't support it. In this case, you should pare away unnecessary words, phrases, or sentences. In the following example, a sentence about green tea simply clutters the paragraph. Compare the revised sentences to see how the author tightened up her essay.

- **Before:** *The day after that, I walked over to my neighbor's house and discussed with her the history of her property. She made us some green tea, which really hit the spot on such a chilly fall day. During the course of our discussion I found out that in the early 1900's the land was part of the sprawling Mitchell dairy farm.*
- **After:** *The day after that, I walked over to my neighbor's house and discussed with her the history of her property; it turned out that in the early 1900's the land was part of the sprawling Mitchell dairy farm.*

Other types of problems may be fixed by reviewing grammar. Check to be sure, for example, that you use the active rather than passive voice. Note the freshness and originality of the second example as compared to the first:

- **Before:** *A moving speech was made by our principal, and there was much grief and love expressed in the tears of Al's friends.*
- **After:** *I listen to our principal make a moving speech, and then saw Al's friends break down as they tried to express their love and grief for him.*

Also look for clichés as you edit. Replace any overused phrases and images with fresh words that are uniquely your own. Consider the following sentence— it seems conscious of the fact that it is boring and unoriginal, as the phrase *behind the scenes* is in quotation marks:

- **Before:** *My interest in an accounting career was inspired predominantly by my parents' business. Throughout my childhood I was exposed to the "behind the scenes" aspects of operating a small family business, and took great interest in the financial components of the operations.*

Take look at the author's revision. The writer reworked the sentences, making them more personal and original, and followed the advice of *showing* rather than simply *telling*. Notice the use of sensory images that bring the reader into the scene.

- **After:** *Some of my earliest memories are of sitting behind the counter in my family's feed store. I would listen to the ring of the cash register, and watch as my mother carefully entered the sales in a large book. I became fascinated with the rows of numbers—a fascination that continues to this day as I plan a career in accounting.*

The goal of editing is to make certain your essay works well on the level of sentences and words. By checking and correcting your writing this closely, you can make your application essay more personal. Eliminate words and phrases that don't work, and add details that show the reader who you are. After successfully completing the editing process, your writing should be fresh and original, and there should be enough variation to keep your audience interested.

Proofreading

The last step in the writing process is to correct any spelling and punctuation errors that you may have made. Good proofreading involves far more than a simple run of spell check and grammar check on your computer. Reliance on these alone to find your errors is a mistake.

That said, they're not a bad place to start. Read the advice for using spell and grammar checks in chapter 6; it will help you use these programs wisely. After you've run them, you'll need to conduct checks of your own to find anything they may have missed.

After completing the proofreading process, it's a great idea at this point to ask at least two other readers to look at your essay. Choose people you know to be good writers and who will pay careful attention when proofreading. Give them each a fresh hard copy of your essay to work on. Whether proofreading yourself, or having another reader check your work, use the strategies provided thus far and consider the following:

- Did you use any words incorrectly? Check the list of commonly confused and mis-used words on page 85.
- Did you use proper punctuation through-out your essay?
- Did you use exclamation points only in dialogue?
- Is there a good balance of contractions
- Do all subjects and verbs agree?
- Are there any double negatives?
- Have all hyphenated and compound words been used correctly?
- If you're recycling your essay, did you change any reference to the school you're applying to?

ADVICE FROM THE PROS

"Being a savvy wordsmith who has total command of syntax, tone, and voice is great. But it doesn't mean you'll write an effective application essay. If your writing is revealing, and can really make a connection with an admissions counselor, you're hitting the mark. Showcasing your rhetorical skills isn't the real point."

—CHRIS AJAMIAN,
CATES Tutoring

Considerations for Electronic and Paper Submissions

Your final step is submitting the essay. Many schools now emphasize that they strongly prefer electronic submissions. Some even waive or reduce their fee to entice you to submit your application online. But the option of completing a paper application is still open at most schools.

What should you do if you have a choice? Hands down—choose the electronic option. Admissions offices are going paperless, and they enjoy the ease of sharing applications electronically. If you do send a paper version, don't expect it to make the rounds of counselors who notice how neatly you filled it out. Once it arrives, your application will be scanned immediately, and look much like the rest.

"I felt I was able to set myself apart and give each school more tailored information. I also thought it was easier to connect with the essay prompts when the school application listed ones that were different than the Common Application."

—MATTHEW FISHMAN,
college freshman

You may also have the choice of completing the Common Application or the school's own. Although admissions counselors often say they have no preference, there can be a slight advantage to using the school's version.

However, if you use the Common

Application, you won't just be making it easier to submit the forms that you must fill out. High school reports, teacher evaluations, mid-year grade reports, and final reports are all electronically sent to where you're applying. Not only does that save time, but it takes some of the worry out of the application process. Therefore, there are fewer details for you to remember and follow through on.

A major complaint about the Common Application—that you must use the same essay for each school—just isn't true. The following procedure will allow you to use different essays, which is especially valuable if you've opted to write a Demonstrated Interest essay:

1. Submit the Common Application to at least one school, then log out of your account.

2. Go to the following website: https://www.commonapp.org/CommonApp/ Default.aspx?allowcopy=true. Enter your existing username and password on the screen and click on *Login*.

3. You will be taken to a screen titled "Common Application," where you'll find information about the application you submitted. Click on *Replicate*, which will make another version of your submitted application. When done, this version will be visible, along with a special drop down in the upper right corner of the application. This will allow access to all of your applications.

4. Upload a new essay to the new version of your application, and connect it to the school(s) you want to receive that essay.

A Word of Warning

Electronic application submission is fast and easy. But fast and easy could mean you don't take the time to check and recheck your work. It's much simpler to click *Send* than it is to print out a number of pages, put them in an envelope, get the proper postage, and put the application in the mail. Unfortunately, students tend to treat everything online more casually than any other type of communication.

If you're submitting your application electronically, keep these potential problems in mind. Proofread for errors—and make sure the application for school A doesn't include any information about school B. The time you invest in making sure your applications are in great shape is time well spent.

PUTTING IT ALL TOGETHER: WHAT WORKS, AND WHAT DOESN'T

The sample student essays in this chapter are included for one important reason: there is much to learn from the strengths and weaknesses of other personal essays. As you read each one, think about what you know about what makes a great essay. Imagine the kinds of comments you think the essays will receive from readers, and take notes in the space provided. As you look at the feedback provided, compare it to your observations. Were the weaknesses you detected the same as those described? Were you able to spot strong introductions, descriptions that weren't vivid enough, or examples of too much telling and not enough showing? The better you become at evaluating other application essays, the more you'll be able to bring to your own work.

Essay One

The tentacles move back and forth, waving at me. Despite being cut up into pieces, the squid is as alive as ever. Do I dare eat it? The atmosphere in the room feels overwhelming, inundated with a toxic mix of humidity and sweat. I sit with my host mother and her two sons in a crowded, yet somehow quiet, age-old restaurant. She picks up a piece of squid with her chopsticks and places it on my plate with an innocent smile. My younger host brother scarfs down his squid. I look at the squid on my plate and it looks back at me as if to say, "Nihon eh youcoso" (Welcome to Japan).

The uneasiness of the moment reminded me of what had happened three long weeks ago...When I met my host family in Japan, the first comment my host mother made was, "Kare wah totemo segatakai amerika jene desu yo" (He is a very tall American). I politely responded, "Hai. Watashi wah roku foot yon inches desu." This combination of English and Japanese translates as, "Yes. Six-feet, four-inches." My host mother—an affable Malaysian cook who met her Japanese husband while he was touring Malaysia during his vacation—didn't answer but merely smiled and shifted her eyes downward. I first thought that she didn't understand my English, but I then realized that she only knew the metric system. After a crude calculation in my head, I said, "Gomenasai, hyaku kyu jyu centimeters desu" (Sorry, 190 centimeters). My host family looked at me—shocked.

Maybe it was my clumsy Japanese, or my very tall stature (I was at least a full foot taller than everyone in the room) that caused the tension, but whatever the reason, the awkwardness in my face was undeniable as my cheeks slowly turned red. My first two weeks in Japan were rife with culture clashes, big and small. I was taught to use only formal language when speaking to strangers and to always be self deprecating when talking about myself. I learned to bow instead of to shake hands. I also learned to not drench my food in soy sauce, but rather to enjoy its simplicity and purity, or as my host mother put it, jyunsui. Looks of disgust were sent my way when I didn't think to shower before entering the local hot spring, or when I didn't offer a name card to people that I met. But, little by little, I chipped away at the mystery that was Japan.

By the end of the second week, I had started to find a place in this different universe, and when my host mother asked me if I would like to visit my older host brother's school, I enthusiastically responded, "Hai!" Upon walking into the school however, I became conscious that I was still wearing my shoes, breaking a cardinal rule in Japan: always take your shoes off when entering a building. I quickly removed my shoes before anyone noticed and donned a pair of mint green slippers—offered by a jovial teacher—that were paper-thin and had a cracked smiley face on the front. Naturally, the slippers were too small and only three of my toes fit. I settled for walking bare foot, only to trigger giggles from a group of kindergarteners who were learning English by playing "paper-scissor-rock." I felt my face getting warm, but I walked over to them, name card in hand.

I chose to go to Japan because I wanted to enrich my ability to speak the language, but by the end of the trip I found so much more. I had transformed from the ignorant red-faced American who forgot to take his shoes off, to the insider ex-pat who knew where to find the best hole-in-the-wall restaurants in Tokyo. I had somehow found a place in this neon-lit and green-tea-obsessed world.

Still wiggling, the tentacle tries to escape the grip of my chopstick. The sweat on my hand almost causes me to drop this Japanese delicacy. My host brothers watch me, waiting to see if the American will truly embrace their world. Hesitating every step of the way, I raise the chopsticks to my mouth. My courage falters, if only for a moment. I thrust the squid in my mouth and chew and chew and chew and quickly swallow. My host family applauds—causing the couple wearing Kimonos next to us to turn around—and I smile.

The squid was not delicious. I did not become more Japanese at this moment. I did learn, however, how a small act of respect can help to bridge the cultural divide.

Your Notes and Reactions

_____

_____

_____

_____

_____

_____

_____

_____

_____

_____

Feedback

Essays about diversity can be tricky; many students' experiences are limited to their own school and surrounding area. Descriptions of people met on volunteer trips, or even on academic trips as the one described in the essay, can easily veer into stereotypes (which can be offensive) or clichés. This essay, however, is an example of how to do it well.

Take note of the opening sentences, which describe a squid. The vivid details draw the reader in without giving too much away. Also notice the way the senses are engaged, helping the reader to further connect with the story. You can almost *hear* the kindergarteners giggling, *see* the tentacles of the squid moving, and *feel* the cheeks of the writer turning red.

Finally, review the conclusion. While the writer does state in an earlier sentence that he went to Japan expecting one outcome and left having learned much more, he doesn't end with that idea, which could simply be a cliché. Instead, he ends by returning to the squid he described in his opening paragraph. The final sentence makes sense of the anecdote without making more of it than necessary.

Essay Two

I clean and relabel the test tubes, put the plates in the 30 degree incubator, turn off the light, and lock the door to the Mount Sinai lab. My dad picks me up, and we drive to the shop that my belly dancing teacher runs. Her husband and my father stay in the small living room, drinking Turkish coffee and chatting while she takes me into the little enchanted room of hip scarves, earrings, head pieces, veils, finger cymbals, and tribal and traditional costumes. We choose a traditional Persian-looking teal and gold costume for me, the beautiful skirt embroidered with a lotus. To be creative we drape gold necklaces from the center top piece to the back. Next, we choose a gold chiffon veil. I let my long hair down.

Walking into the living room to show my father, I shyly unwrap the veil from my body, and at that moment I feel truly sacred. My father always says I have an old soul, and at that moment I understand completely—I feel united with my female ancestors, that I am continuing something magical. To define me as a belly dancer or a scientist is insufficient; I am both.

It was always a given that I would pursue science. To me, science, specifically biological research, is an intricate puzzle. I enjoy the intense focus required to perform an abstruse procedure, like cutting bands of E.coli DNA and ligating it through electrophoresis. I am able to tune out any distractions and find it peaceful to focus on the task at hand. It is fascinating to think how a million different complicated molecular processes are tiny expressions that combine to form the complex language of life. Being able to speak that language gives me a sense of pride and empowerment. I realize that just as in dance, here too there is an unveiling. But here it is the contents of my mind that are revealed.

The language of belly dancing, in contrast, is a silent celebration of a woman's body and her connection to ancestors, nature, and life. This is a language that I am equally proud to speak. Belly dancing brings me back to my roots. When I dance, I feel connected to my Persian ancestors, and I am remembering and honoring their existence through the movement of my body. I think of my Aunt Touran in home videos tenderly holding my father as a child. I imagine grown-ups watching belly dancers at family events and parties. So belly dancing not only reminds me of my heritage, but also of the joys of being with family. Whenever or wherever I hear Middle Eastern music, my body instantly reacts—excitement rushes through my veins, my eyes widen, and I smile. I love the intricate motion of my hands when dancing, the tension I hold in them; in the full body movement there is sensuality and grace.

Biological research and belly dancing may seem like an unusual combination, but to me it makes perfect sense. Belly dancing offers me a figurative entranceway to my past, and science offers me greater insight into the basics of life and the potential of the future. It is in balancing these two contrasting passions that I can discover who I am and what makes me happy. There is an unveiling to my own self; discovering what my body can do and what my mind can create. I feel my whole body dances cohesively and fervently with movements of the past and ambitions of the future.

Your Notes and Reactions

Feedback

Although this essay might have used as its subject something that was already mentioned elsewhere on the student's application (the fact that she has studied belly dancing for six years), it isn't always a recipe for failure. Here, the writer reveals much more about herself, through her discussion of belly dancing, then could ever be conveyed in a simple list. The strong connection with family and ancestry highlighted in the essay also shows that this student is coming from a supportive environment, one she is proud of and that has provided a stable base from which she can grow.

In addition, she has made some unique connections between her love of dancing and science. Both are described as having languages of their own, each providing a type of unveiling, which helps the writer understand more about herself. Through the clever juxtaposition of these two seemingly different passions, she is able to tell the reader much more about herself than a mere mention of an activity and a potential major.

Essay Three

The kitchen table is the chaotic Wall Street of my home. It easily beats out the upstairs bathroom shared by two teenage girls. It defeats the computer, which all five family members fight over to send messages to other friends. It surpasses the family room, with the main television, and one remote.

As the sun goes down, we trickle to the table after assembling our plates. As soon as the last members lower themselves into their chairs, the conversation erupts, usually with me. I am the oldest child in the family and the one who always has something to share. It also helps that I am the first to the table and the first to finish eating. Soon the table has exploded with conversation and laughter. Everyone wants to say what happened in their day. What funny thing the biology teacher said today. What a friend said in the hall. Anything and everything mildly funny or sad that occurred in our lives during the day is applicable to the conversation.

Ironically, everyone wants to share everything that happens to them, yet they care less who is listening. And so, our dinner conversations morph into a competitive exchange between the stories and the voices of all at the table. If you can't keep up, you might as well shut up.

These "conversations" are the best part of my day. The average six days a week I get to have them are priceless. Although a specifically earth shattering volume and persistence is necessary to survive, it is the one time that the true chemistry of my family comes together. Like these conversations, I live from one laughing moment to the next. As soon as I finish my last laugh, I wait hungrily for the next. I am told my laughter is contagious, and I love to hear other people laughing along with me.

My family and the time I spend with them, is a strong base for me. We laugh together, cry together, grow together, and of course, eat together. I often stay home on Friday nights to spend time with my family. My family supports me in everything I do, and is the backbone of my success thus far, and I know with them behind me I will go farther. Without my thirteen-year-old brother's attempts at telling stories, my father's inabilities to remember names, or even my sister's incessant voice-cracks, my life would not be the same.

As I leave this table, I know that I will have my family behind me, and this experience will be one I can share. I know I will bring this constant jabber with me wherever I go. Every time I sit to eat in my new and larger kitchen, it will remind me of my old debate arena, as the daily events spill onto the table.

Your Notes and Reactions

_____

_____

_____

_____

_____

_____

_____

_____

_____

_____

_____

_____

_____

Feedback

Here is an example of the writer's magnifying lens at work. Many students choose to write about their families, and the subject reveals some important concepts. Remember that admissions counselors are looking for students who can not only handle college-level academic work, but who are also mature and stable enough to handle life on their own, make new friends, and contribute to the community. This essay makes readers think that the writer is indeed ready for college.

This student, although she has not been part of a household in China and doesn't have a heritage that led her to an exotic activity such as belly dancing, has focused in on an important element of family life. Some writers gripe that their experiences aren't unique enough to make them stand out in an essay, but this essay demonstrates that the magnifying lens that brings an activity into sharper and more personal focus can take a subject from the common to the highly personal and poignant.

Essay Four

The smell of freshness amongst the midnight skies, a crisp taste we all dream about, wind streaming by sounding like a mini tornado over the ear drums, only the sun's reflection of the moon lighting up above, as darkness swirls around the solo motorcycle. Suddenly! Buzz...Buzz... Buzz... a vibration then comes from my friend's pockets. His right hand releases the throttle, leaving the left hand struggling against pot holes in the dark.

SMACK!...RING...RING...RING...the phone at 2:30 am. "Hello Mrs. Cleary, this is Jane at City Hospital. Your son was just in a motorcycle accident and we would like for you and your family to come to the emergency room immediately." In a matter of minutes the family of five frantically raced to the E.R. Hearts pumping, neurons running through the nerve cells like blind mice knowing what to think, they arrived. There he was, lying on the E.R. bed, legs crossed, blood covering his face, a site each and every family should never see. Tears pouring down their faces as they said their goodbyes. Then all of a sudden the doctor saw his left leg twitch and yelled "FLY HIM TO UNIVERSITY HOSPITAL...HES GOT A CHANCE TO LIVE!!"

Scary enough, three months in a comma and 6 months in ICU, we thought my friend was a goner. All of the impact focused on his forehead and skull, and the doctors assumed that there could be severe brain damage with a possibility of being mentally screwed up. With the support we gave and his own inner ambitions Patrick survived the miracle without any internal damage. Each and every human in this world deserves the same amount of respect, whether they be two years old or seventy years old Japanese man.

Since up to this age of the accident, 14 years old, I only knew of "old" people who died. Older people who have health issues that make them slowly parish. When looking upon my friend's closed eyes, who was tangled in life support tubes, I got my first glimpse of death. For three months we lived in tearer of a fear that he might go. For three months I was lost within my brain, looking for a conclusion to my situation; having the feeling to act foolish as I did not know how to react. I have come to realize that life is short, to look and act with everyone as if it was their last moment.

Your Notes and Reactions

_____

_____

_____

_____

_____

_____

_____

_____

_____

_____

Feedback

Because it's important, many students think they must write an application essay that's dramatic. If they've experienced a death of a family member or friend, or an accident such as the one described in Essay Four, they conclude that it's the right subject for the essay. But big and bold doesn't necessarily mean successful.

You probably noted some of the many errors in word choice, grammar, and punctuation throughout this essay. References to potential mental problems and Japanese men may have stood out as potentially offensive. The long, dramatic description of a cold, dark night might have also caught your attention. But the real problem is a more fundamental one: the essay reveals almost nothing about the writer.

The only hint we get of the person behind this essay is a cliché: who doesn't, at least for a while, view life as more precious when they are faced with a loss? Rather than revise, edit, and proofread, this student needs to go back to his personal inventory to find a story that reveals something about him. The opportunity to make a connection with the reader shouldn't be missed by focusing on a subject that, no matter how dramatic, says little about the writer.

Essay Five

Sunday. As the bus bumps along through the muggy heat of July, I find it hard to be proud. Although I have just played great soccer in the Eastern Regional Tournament and am on my way to Regional Camp, to compete with sixty other girls for positions on the East Coast Select Team, I feel tremendously nervous and inferior. The hot bus ride has been lengthened from five to nine miserable hours, and I already think that everyone at the camp will be much better than I am. Yet when I call my parents that night and learn that my grandmother has had a second stroke and is in the hospital, I realize that this week of competition is going to be much more challenging emotionally than physically.

Wednesday. I haven't been playing very well; I'm on the reserve team and my chances for advancement are slim. There is only one person who can alleviate my depression: my mother. Somehow she already knows just what to say. That night, I call her to say hello and let her cheer me up. Instead, she tells me that my grandmother is now in a coma. The news hits me like a physical blow. My mind starts reeling with thoughts of my grandmother: the way she would pour her coffee into water glasses if it wasn't scalding hot, her soft, all-encompassing bear hugs, her smiling voice over the phone. The thought of this plump, joyful woman I love so much lying prone on a cold, sterile hospital bed is too painful to think about, so I lose myself in a fantasy novel.

Thursday morning. Now I'm really playing poorly; my mind is with my grandmother, not my soccer ball. I look up across the field and see my whole family clustered together, walking slowly towards me. I know. Before I realize what I'm doing, tears are streaming down my face as I choke sobs into my mother's hair.

Thursday afternoon. The funeral service is over, and I'm struggling to come to terms with what has happened, trying to accept the fact that I will never see my grandmother again, except in faded pictures and fond memories. I go into a bedroom to talk to my aunt, and oh what strength it takes for me to hold her and try to comfort and sooth her as she breaks down and cries into my hair. I realize that even though she is 36 and I am 14, I have to be the adult. My aunt is single; she has no close family left except my mother and my uncle, while I still have both my parents, two brothers, and a sister. I cannot imagine how deep her grief must be, and know no words that will make it go away, so I remain silent, wondering how I will feel when my mother dies.

Friday, a little after 11:00 am. After much debate, I have decided to return to the Regional Camp for the last game. My grandmother would have wanted me to finish what I'd started, even though she never quite understood our family's obsession with soccer. I also feel I have an obligation to myself to follow through: I have worked so hard and so long to get to this point that I would be letting myself down if I didn't grasp my last opportunity to be selected. The coaches put me on the advanced team, the only one they really watch, and I block out all thoughts of my grandmother and play my heart out—for fifteen minutes. The game ends. Regional Camp is over, and I haven't made the team. Another blow. This is the first time someone has told me I'm not good enough at soccer and it hurts. I resolve to work harder.

Friday afternoon. I am on my way home, staring out the car window, seeing yet not seeing the trees rush by. As I reflect back on the events of these past few days, I find that my focus isn't on my failure to make the team. I think about how I've been able to help my aunt with her sorrow, and to overcome my own grief and continue to strive for success.

Your Notes and Reactions

_____

_____

_____

_____

_____

_____

_____

_____

_____

_____

_____

_____

_____

Feedback

Although this is an example of another dramatic essay, this one doesn't fall victim to the problems of the previous one. While it is about the writer's grandmother's death, it also manages to do much more. By using the backdrop of soccer tryouts, she is able to show the reader a glimpse of herself. What do we learn? Most importantly, that she comes from a strong family, she sometimes doubts her abilities but doesn't give up, and she's empathetic.

Her family's loss is also not described in overly-dramatic language, which is often a temptation for this subject. While obviously not upbeat, the tone isn't completely somber, either. The writer also uses an interesting and effective organization that grabs the reader's attention. The essay is broken down into scenarios which are ordered chronologically. Finally, it centers on a situation in which the end result wasn't a success, without making the writer seem like a failure (in fact, she may not have mentioned this soccer tryout on her application because of the result, but it works in the essay).

Essay Six

Walking down Old Stage Road, an elderly couple spotted a vehicle with a curious appendage. As the car drew nearer, the couple saw what appeared to be a human head sticking far out of one of the windows. Upon passing, they determined this head belonged to a boy of about nine, with a pale look on his face.

That nine year-old boy was me. Riding in the backseat of our family minivan, I was as nervous as can be. The waves of nausea that cascaded over me forced my body to seek refuge in the fresh air outside, resulting in the single rolled down window that made everyone's ears shake. With palms sweating and knees shaking, we arrived at the building where my very first piano recital was to take place.

As it turns out, that evening went surprisingly well. No stumble on the endless walk to the stage, no blaring mistakes, and a well-executed bow were among my most notable achievements. But none of this discounts the difficulty that performing in front of an audience presents. Being a fairly shy person, this aspect of playing the piano was very difficult.

However, performing wasn't the only obstacle I encountered when beginning my piano career. As an athletic kid growing up in an athletic family, I found that the learning curve of most sports was steep in the beginning and then shallowed-out over time. But as I became more accomplished at the piano, the learning curve flipped. In the first few years, I could learn pieces in less than an hour, and memorize them before my next weekly lesson. By high school though, pieces required weeks of daily practice in order to make any progress. I wasn't used to this system and, being a bit of a perfectionist, I became very frustrated. I would throw childish hissy fits, bending the spines of my books in the process. I was more than ready to quit.

But that wasn't the end. More setbacks came my way. When my meathead-like friends found out that the reason why I was leaving early from lacrosse practice once a week was for piano lessons, the floodgates opened and the torrent of liquid demoralizer rushed in. The middle school "nerd jokes" hit me very hard, even bringing me to tears sometimes. I was so embarrassed to be playing the piano that I refused to go to my lessons and I asked my mother to let me quit.

This could have been the end of the line, but my mom wouldn't let me quit. I was the only family member still playing my great-grandmother's piano, and my mom didn't want her father's post-war gift to his mother to become cold with retirement after all its years of life. I fought and fought, to no avail. Piano lessons continued. And I'm so glad they did.

Now that I'm older, I thank my mom every day for not letting me quit. Playing the piano has become an artistic passion of mine that I had never imagined would. Of course I still experience the nervousness of performing, the torture of the learning curve, and the occasional joke, but none of that matters to me anymore. I look at performing as a way to let people know what I'm capable of; the pain of the beginning of the learning curve as a step toward the joy that comes when the arc steepens; the taunting as an indicator of what I've been able to accomplish as an athletic teenager.

As busy as I've been throughout high school, I've had more reasons to quit than ever, but I can't imagine giving up piano. When I sit down and my fingers start tickling the ivories, the world stops. All the worries of a high school senior get pushed to the back of my brain to make room for the feeling of freedom that ensues. This is when I know that as hard as life gets, I will never give up playing the piano.

Your Notes and Reactions

_____

_____

_____

_____

_____

_____

_____

_____

_____

_____

_____

_____

_____

Feedback

This essay demonstrates that its writer possesses most of the traits listed on the Common Application Teacher Recommendation Form, including creativity, motivation, and disciplined work habits. Its introduction hooks the reader with an image of a young boy's head hanging out a car window. And while you may have questioned the writer's decision to delve into old childhood memories (which often don't reveal much about who a student is today), this essay moves quickly into the present, connecting the piano lessons of earlier years to more challenging recent ones.

Errors that should be corrected for the final version of this essay include a few repetitions (the word *quit* appears five times, for example), and the reference to "nerd jokes" (substituting *middle school* would get the point across just as well while eliminating the risk of offending the reader). At over 650 words, the essay is also too long for some schools. Notice that the first three paragraphs describe the first piano recital. They could easily be condensed. The last two paragraphs both sound like conclusions, and some tightening could be done there without a loss of important details or insights.

Essay Seven

I vividly remember the time I first heard the poem "The Dash". I was still a boy, in 7th grade, and I was in an elementary school gym having basketball practice with my traveling team. Practice was almost over so, as you can imagine, my teammates and I were a little anxious to leave. We lost focus. My Coach, Jim Harrison, huddled us up at center court, and told us to take a seat. Being 7th graders, we moaned and complained under our breath about having to stay an extra couple minutes.

Coach Harrison pulled out a piece of paper from his back pocket and unfolded it. The gym immediately turned quiet, we knew he had something to say. He began to read us this poem, an unusual thing for a coach to do at a basketball practice. I was listening very closely to each line. The words struck home deep down in my heart. I could feel what the writer was communicating. I was changed by that poem; my attitude and philosophy would never be the same.

The poem called "The Dash" was written by Notre Dame football player Alton Maiden. The poem is about the dash in-between the date of birth and the date of death on a gravestone. Maiden wrote, "People may forget your birth and death, but they will never forget your dash." The dash represents people's lives, what they did in their lifetime. I have always tried to do the right thing, and give my best in whatever I am doing.

When I'm playing sports I think about the dash. I always give 110 percent to make my teammates and myself better. My best friends are my teammates and I work hard for them because I know they do the same for me. In the long run, I don't want to be remembered as an outstanding athlete or a great player, but as a hard worker who never gave up. Sports, while very important, are just one of many things in my dash.

I wasn't exactly sure how to name this next part of the dash, but I think a good name for it is sharing. Sharing is something I always try to do. During the summer I work at a camp as a counselor. I do it because I love sharing my time to make a difference in those kids' lives. I cry tears of happiness every summer knowing these kids will never forget the week they spent at Camp Destiny and their time with me. I am volunteering every week as a Big Brother/Big Sister working with a 6th grade student. He has a learning disability and is bi-polar. Although I am supposed to be teaching him, he is teaching me, showing me how to appreciate what I have and how true happiness is found only in one's heart. Sharing is an amazing gift because it is not only a huge chunk of my dash, it is something that makes other people's dashes better.

As high school ends and I am looking at colleges, I want to make sure I continue filling my dash. Your college will help in my pursuit for a strong dash. The satisfaction of facing the challenges that a top notch school like yours has to offer will inspire me to keep working my hardest. It will continue shaping me into a better person, with its wide variety of learning experiences.

My dash is something that I hold close to my heart because I know that it's the only thing I will really care about in the end. It won't matter how many points I scored, money I made, songs I recorded, or the grade point average I achieved. The experiences I've had in this life and what I got out of them is what really matters. I hope others will think of me as a hard, determined worker who always tries to do the right thing. I know that as long as I put forth my best effort in whatever I am doing, the dash will take care of itself.

Your Notes and Reactions

Feedback

Remember, the personal essay is your opportunity to sell yourself to a college. In many ways, it's an integral part of a marketing campaign—and you're the product. But there's a fine line between revealing something positive and sounding boastful. This essay does the latter, especially in the paragraph about volunteering. While this student may be honest about his effect on others, and about the tears he sheds, the overall effect is a turn-off. And the line "he's teaching me more than I'm teaching him," while possibly true, is clichéd.

You may have noted that paragraph five, while intended to demonstrate interest, offers no specific reasons as to why the student is applying, or what the college could actually offer him. Any student could have written it about any school. Length is another problem with this essay. Think about how you would rewrite the first paragraph to retain many of the details while getting to the point more quickly.

Finally, recall the show versus tell distinction. After the first paragraph, which uses about 120 words before mentioning the poem, there are very few concrete details. What does "giving 110 percent" mean? What does the writer do as a counselor at Camp Destiny that is so unforgettable? The essay would be greatly improved with more showing.

Essay Eight

I first realized I belong at Pomona College while speaking with a recent alumni. I was enthralled to learn that Pomona would host a Death by Chocolate "pre-finals frenzy" for students. And I took it as a sign. Upon a closer look, I discovered that there were many other signs that made Pomona the perfect fit. Primarily, Pomona would provide the personal intellectual foundation essential for "a rewarding and productive life in a rapidly changing world."

As a passionate student, I have always had an enthusiastic and resilient approach to learning and a desire to broaden my knowledge across many disciplines. As a responsible individual, I have always been driven to forge my own path. Pomona's *Breadth of Study Requirements* are particularly fitting for me for these reasons. I value the flexibility in course selection and the opportunity to explore a wide range of fields. I'm the type of student who would take economics, statistics, and Chinese even if they weren't distribution requirements.

I also appreciate Pomona's emphasis on skillful writing ability and intellectual thinking in the *Critical Inquiry* seminars. I look forward to the mentorship available and to such fascinating topics as *Pilgrimage, Travel and Cultural Encounter; Cultural Psychology; Fairy Tales; The TV Novel;* and *Finding India.* I find interdisciplinary study to be the most invigorating and rewarding.

I am interested in pursuing a major in *Media Studies.* I hope to develop my ability to thoroughly analyze media across cultures, time periods, and perspectives. I anticipate expanding my knowledge on diverse media and evaluating them from multiple disciplinary angles. I am eager to obtain hands-on experience, as well.

Beyond the rigorous and engaging academics, another factor that makes Pomona shine above all other colleges is the campus life. Although I was not able to make the cross-country trip for a campus visit, I have done extensive research, and from what I learned from Pomona students themselves, I feel that I can truly identify with them, especially their open-mindedness and collaborative nature. I hope to participate in the *International Club, On the Loose Outing Club,* and *Harmony* multicultural newspaper. I would also like to start a collegiate figure skating club.

I know myself well; I am aware of what bolsters my spirit and what hinders it. I know that my opportunities for growth are amplified when I have access to the most challenging material and when I am surrounded by the most productive people. Pomona College provides the best environment for me, inside the classroom and out; an environment where I can become more than the enterprising, compassionate, and gregarious student I am now, to become a person of influence. But, of course, Pomona had me at chocolate.

Your Notes and Reactions

_____

_____

_____

_____

_____

_____

_____

_____

_____

Feedback

This essay was written for a short-answer prompt named "Why Pomona?" You'll recall that many schools include similar demonstrated interest topics, and you can also include an essay of this type on the Common Application as your topic of choice (follow the directions in chapter 7 to use different essays for each school to which you're applying).

While this student was not able to base her essay on information gathered through direct contact, she clearly made the most of the resources available to her, and was able to describe a number of specific reasons why she was applying to Pomona.

While the ending of this essay is humorous, and you've received words of warning about using humor, it's an example of what works. The reference here to chocolate works well for a number of reasons. First, it reveals something fun about the writer, a detail that balances the seriousness of academic rigor. Second, it ties back to the essay's opening. Third, it shows the effort this student made to learn about Pomona. She didn't rely solely on the Internet or marketing materials published by the school. Even without a campus visit, she spoke with a recent alumni, gathered information from available resources, and created an essay that works.

COLLEGE ADMISSIONS RESOURCES

Online Resources

As you begin to plan for college, make the most of the following online resources to plan successfully.

Testing

To learn more about standardized tests, including what's on them, when they're offered, and how to register, look no further than the official sources themselves (be careful, other sites may contain information that isn't accurate): www.collegeboard.com (SAT) and www.act.org (ACT). Both sites have practice questions, practice tests, and advice for achieving a higher score. If you're taking the SAT, be sure to sign up for the SAT Question of the Day—this can be delivered to your inbox every morning, and the site will even keep track of your results.

Don't like your test scores? There are hundreds of test-optional schools that don't require your scores. For a list of these schools, check out www.fairtest.org.

General Admissions Process

Find out what's on the minds of college admissions counselors at www.nacacnet. org. The National Association of College Admissions Counseling is made up of those who make crucial admissions decisions, and they share their preferences and experiences in an annual survey. The Student Resources page has a link to buy their *Guide for Parents*—also worth a look.

Finding a School

There are dozens of college guides available online, and the accuracy of information varies widely. If you're into rankings, read first about how they're compiled before you rely on them too heavily. If you have some parameters in mind, such as location, size, or major, search sites such as www.petersons.com, www.princetonreview.com, and www.collegeboard.com.

Other sites offer feedback from current students and have message boards where you can share and ask for information and advice. These include: www.collegeconfidential.com and www.collegeprowler.com.

When looking at individual schools' sites, keep in mind that they are designed as marketing tools. The students all look smart, engaged, and fun; and every blade of grass appears to have been manicured by hand. You will get comprehensive information about majors, professors, application dates, and activities, but don't make a decision solely based on the visuals—or the glowing comments or descriptions.

Paying for School

Get sound financial advice and apply for federal aid at www.finaid.org. You can get information about loans, scholarships, and savings options. There's also a college cost projector and savings plan designer to help you determine what you can afford.

Books

The number of books on college admissions is staggering, and grows daily! While many offer sound advice, they really vary in quality. And some—especially those that promise to get you into a highly selective school—aren't worth your time. The following books are among the most up-to-date and reliable sources of information.

General Guides

Fiske Guide to Colleges 2010 (Fiske) is highly recommended; it goes beyond statistics and describes school environments with astounding accuracy. One important rule for any book you're considering is to check the publication date. Most guides are updated annually, and for good reason. Buy only the most recent version.

Four-Year College 2010 (Peterson's) provides comprehensive information on every accredited four-year institution in the United States and Canada (where you'll find some amazing bargains).

Targeted Info Guide

Colleges that Change Lives: 40 Schools that Will Change the Way you Think About Colleges (Penguin) was groundbreaking when it came out over a decade ago, and now (revised and updated) it's a classic. If you can't get beyond brand name paralysis, here's where to start.

General Admissions Process Guides

A Is for Admission: The Insider's Guide to Getting into the Ivy League and Other Top Colleges (Grand Central) gives valuable advice from an industry insider on what really goes on in the admissions offices of highly selective schools. Michele Hernandez reveals the mathematical formula used to rank applicants, and offers advice for raising yours.

The New Rules of College Admissions: Ten Former Admissions Officers Reveal What it Takes to Get Into College Today (Fireside) offers sound advice that covers a wide range of topics (extracurricular activities, choosing a college, interviews, recommendations). For a broad understanding of the general admissions process, it's a great place to start.

Finances

Paying for College Without Going Broke 2010 (Princeton Review) is a great resource for getting a good deal on a college education. This book covers much more than just financial aid, including understanding how to get tax breaks, negotiating with schools (yes, it can work!), and planning ahead to save before you begin the application process.

Test Practice

The folks who make the ACT and SAT exams offer actual retired tests so you can gauge your progress. *The Official SAT Study Guide* (College Board) and *The Real*

ACT Prep Guide (Peterson's) are a great way to practice. But these companies don't give too much away. For explanations of question types and strategies, you'll need to look elsewhere.

In-Depth Test Strategy

Don't overlook the importance of understanding how admissions tests are designed to make you stumble, and how to outsmart them. *Up Your Score: The Underground Guide to the SAT* (Workman Publishing) and *ACT Preparation in a Flash* (LearningExpress) are the books to turn to for solid test strategy.

COLLEGES THAT ACCEPT THE COMMON APPLICATION

The following schools accept the Common Application (at the time of this book's printing):

Adelphi University
Agnes Scott College
Albion College
Albright College
Alfred University
Allegheny College
American University
Amherst College
Arcadia University
Assumption College
Augsburg College
Augustana College - Illinois
Augustana College - South Dakota
Austin College
Babson College

Baldwin-Wallace College
Bard College
Barnard College
Bates College
Belmont University
Beloit College
Bennington College
Bentley University
Berry College
Birmingham-Southern College
Boston College
Boston University
Bowdoin College
Bradley University
Brandeis University

Brown University
Bryant University
Bryn Mawr College
Bucknell University
Burlington College
Butler University
Cabrini College
California Inst of Technology (Caltech)
California Lutheran University
Canisius College
Carleton College
Carnegie Mellon University
Carroll College (Montana)

Case Western Reserve University

The Catholic University of America

Cazenovia College

Cedar Crest College

Centenary College of Louisiana

Centre College

Champlain College

Chapman University

Chatham College

Claremont McKenna College

Clark University

Clarkson University

Coe College

Colby College

Colby-Sawyer College

Colgate University

The College of Idaho

College of Mount Saint Vincent

*The College of New Jersey

College of New Rochelle

College of St. Benedict (St. John's University)

College of the Atlantic

College of the Holy Cross

*College of William & Mary

College of Wooster

Colorado College

*Colorado State University

Columbia College Chicago

Concordia College - New York

Connecticut College

Converse College

Cornell College

Cornell University

Creighton University

Curry College

Daemen College

Dartmouth College

Davidson College

Denison University

DePauw University

Dickinson College

Dominican University of California

Dowling College

Drake University

Drew University

Drexel University

Duke University

Earlham College

Eckerd College

Elizabethtown College

Elmira College

Emerson College

Emmanuel College

Emory University

Erskine College

Fairfield University

Fisk University

Florida Southern College

Fordham University

Franklin & Marshall College

Franklin Pierce University

Franklin W. Olin College of Engineering

Furman University

George Fox University

The George Washington University

Gettysburg College

Gonzaga University

Goucher College

Green Mountain College

Grinnell College

Guilford College

Gustavus Adolphus College

Hamilton College

Hamline University

Hampden-Sydney College

Hampshire College

Hanover College

Hartwick College

Harvard College

Harvey Mudd College

Haverford College

Hendrix College

Hillsdale College

Hiram College

Hobart & William Smith Colleges

Hofstra University

Hollins University

Hood College

Hope College

Illinois College

Illinois Institute of Technology

Illinois Wesleyan University

Immaculata University
Iona College
Ithaca College
John Carroll University
Johns Hopkins
  University
Juniata College
Kalamazoo College
*Keene State College
Kenyon College
Keystone College
King's College
Knox College
La Salle University
Lafayette College
Lake Erie College
Lake Forest College
Lasell College
Lawrence Technological
  University
Lawrence University
Lees-McRae College
Lehigh University
LeMoyne College
Lesley College
Lewis & Clark College
Linfield College
List College, The Jewish
  Theological Seminary
Long Island University
  - C.W. Post Campus
Loyola Marymount
  University
Loyola University
  Maryland
Loyola University New
  Orleans
Luther College
Lycoming College

Lynn University
Macalester College
Manhattan College
Manhattanville College
Marietta College
Marist College
Marlboro College
Marquette University
Marymount Manhattan
  College
Maryville College
Maryville University of
  St. Louis
Massachusetts College
  of Pharmacy &
  Health Sciences
McDaniel College
Menlo College
Mercyhurst College
Meredith College
Merrimack College
*Miami University
  (Ohio)
Middlebury College
Mills College
Millsaps College
Moravian College
Morehouse College
Mount Holyoke College
Mount St. Mary's College
Muhlenberg College
Naropa University
Nazareth College
*New College of Florida
New England College
New School University
  - Eugene Lang College
New York Institute of
  Technology

New York University
Newbury College
Niagara University
Nichols College
Northeastern University
Northland College
Northwestern
  University
Notre Dame de Namur
  University
Oberlin College
Occidental College
Oglethorpe University
Ohio Northern
  University
Ohio Wesleyan
  University
Oklahoma City
  University
Pace University
Pacific Lutheran
  University
Pacific University
Pepperdine University
Philadelphia University
Pitzer College
*Plymouth State
  University
Polytechnic Institute of
  New York University
Pomona College
Presbyterian College
Prescott College
Princeton University
Providence College
Quinnipiac University
Randolph College
Randolph-Macon
  College

Reed College
Regis College
Regis University
Rensselaer Polytechnic
    Institute
Rhodes College
Rice University
*Richard Stockton
    College of New
    Jersey
Rider University
Ringling College of Art
    & Design
Ripon College
Rochester Institute of
    Technology
Roger Williams
    University
Rollins College
Rosemont College
Russell Sage College
Sacred Heart University
Sage College of Albany
Saint Anselm College
St. Bonaventure
    University
St. Catherine University
St. Edward's University
Saint Francis University
St. John Fisher College
Saint Joseph's College
Saint Joseph's
    University
St. John's University
    (College of St.
    Benedict)
St. Lawrence University
Saint Leo University
Saint Louis University

Saint Mary's College of
    California
Saint Mary's College of
    Indiana
Saint Mary's University
    of Minnesota
Saint Michael's College
St. Norbert College
St. Olaf College
Saint Peter's College
St. Thomas Aquinas
    College
Saint Vincent College
Salem College
Salve Regina University
Santa Clara University
Sarah Lawrence College
Scripps College
Seattle Pacific University
Seattle University
Seton Hall University
Seton Hill University
Sewanee: The
    University of the
    South
Siena College
Simmons College
Skidmore College
Smith College
Southern Methodist
    University
Southern New
    Hampshire
    University
Southwestern
    University
Spelman College
Spring Hill College
Stanford University

*SUNY Binghamton
    University
*SUNY Buffalo State
    College
*SUNY College at
    Brockport
*SUNY College at
    Geneseo
*SUNY College at
    Oneonta
*SUNY College of
    Environmental
    Science& Forestry
*SUNY Cortland
*SUNY Fredonia
*SUNY New Paltz
*SUNY Oswego
*SUNY Plattsburgh
*SUNY Purchase
    College
*SUNY Stony Brook
    University
*SUNY University at
    Albany
*SUNY University at
    Buffalo
Stetson University
Stevens Institute of
    Technology
Stevenson University
Stonehill College
Suffolk University
Susquehanna University
Swarthmore College
Sweet Briar College
Syracuse University
Texas Christian
    University
Thiel College

Thomas College
Transylvania University
Trinity College
Trinity University
Tufts University
Union College
University of Chicago
University of Dallas
University of Dayton
*University of Delaware
University of Denver
University of Findlay
University of Great Falls
University of LaVerne
*University of Maine
*University of Maine at
  Farmington
*University of Maine at
  Machias
*University of Mary
  Washington
*University of
  Massachusetts
  Amherst
*University of
  Massachusetts
  Boston
*University of
  Massachusetts
  Dartmouth
*University of
  Massachusetts Lowell
University of Miami
University of New
  England

*University of New
  Hampshire
University of New Haven
University of Notre
  Dame
University of
  Pennsylvania
University of Portland
University of Puget
  Sound
University of Redlands
*University of Rhode
  Island
University of Richmond
University of Rochester
University of San Diego
University of San
  Francisco
University of Scranton
*University of Southern
  Maine
University of Tampa
University of the Pacific
University of Tulsa
*University of Vermont
*University of Virginia
Ursinus College
Utica College
Valparaiso University
Vanderbilt University
Vassar College
Villanova University
Virginia Wesleyan
  College
Wabash College

Wagner College
Wake Forest University
Washington & Jefferson
  College
Washington and Lee
  University
Washington College
Washington University
  in St. Louis
Webster University
Wellesley College
Wells College
Wentworth Institute of
  Technology
Wesleyan University
Westminster College -
  Missouri
Westminster College
  - Pennsylvania
Westminster College -
  Utah
Wheaton College
Wheelock College
Whitman College
Whittier College
Willamette University
William Jewell College
Williams College
Wilson College
Wittenberg University
Wofford College
Worcester Polytechnic
  Institute
Xavier University
Yale University

*denotes a public institution

ADDITIONAL ONLINE PRACTICE ▶

Whether you need help building basic skills or preparing for an exam, visit the LearningExpress Practice Center! On this site, you can access additional practice materials. Using the code below, you'll be able to log in and complete two instantly scored essays online. This online essay practice provides you with:

- **Immediate Scoring**
- **A detailed scoring guide**
- **Personalized recommendations for further practice and study**

Log on to the LearningExpress Practice Center by using the URL: **www.learnatest.com/practice**

This is your Access Code: **7274**

Follow the steps online to redeem your access code. After you've used your access code to register with the site, you will be prompted to create a username and password. For easy reference, record them here:

Username: _____ **Password:** _____

With your username and password, you can log in and answer these practice questions as many times as you like. If you have any questions or problems, please contact LearningExpress customer service at 1-800-295-9556 ext. 2, or e-mail us at **customerservice@learningexpressllc.com**